SANTERÍA
FORMULARY & SPELLBOOK
A GUIDE TO NATURE'S MAGIC

CARLOS MONTENEGRO

ORIGINAL PUBLICATIONS

SANTERIA

Magical Formulary & Spellbook

© 1994 Carlos Galdiano Montenegro

ISBN: 0-942272-52-8

Original Publications
P.O. Box 236
Old Bethpage, New York 11804-0236
1-888-OCCULT-1

Printed in the United States of America

INTRODUCTION

If you were to imagine yourself standing in the middle of a jungle, what would you see? Tall trees, rippling streams or perhaps strange animals nestled amongst exotic plants and brilliantly colored flowers? All of these elements compose of what we call nature, and everything in nature contains power. This power when harnessed correctly produces what is known as natural magic. Natural magic is the manipulation of organic materials found in nature to achieve a desired result.

This form of magic is commonly found in West Africa and the Caribbean. The belief in natural magic is shared not only by myself, but by millions who are participants of the Afro Caribbean religion known as Santeria.

Like many of my books, this one was written as a *"How to"* book for individuals who are active participants in the Santeria Religion. The reason for writing this particular book is to introduce and encourage individuals of Santeria to familiarize themselves with an inexpensive way of preparing the basic ingredients. However, combining natural ingredients alone will not produce the desired effect. In fact, without knowledge of the Santeria Orishas (Saints) and their many paths, the intended results could reverse negatively or perhaps not work at all.

Because we have become a world of blind consumers, it is my concern that the "Buyer Beware" when choosing those natural ingredients that are pure and prepared properly. Common sense tells us that the most basic ingredients can be found for free in nature if we take the time to look for them. Other ingredients may be costly, but if you purchase separate items in a Botanica (Spanish Religious Supply Store), the overall cost will be much cheaper than a fully prepared product. Weak, mass produced commercial products such as: colored floor washes, scented powders and other items are manufactured cost effectively for the producer, not for the consumer.

Rarely is careful attention paid to the preparation of homemade magic products in these modern times. Rarer still, if finding an individual who is dedicated and competent in this aspect of spell crafting. It is a magical institution that is dying and must not be overlooked or forgotten. Making homemade products is a lengthy process, but the success of amagical spell or ritual demands patience and faith.It is my hope that this book will be an important resource guide to the magic found within nature. If properly utilized with respect and reverence, the Santeria practitioner will live harmoniously in nature with the Orishas. It is my hope that this book will be an important resource guide to the magic found within nature. If properly utilized with respect and reverence, the Santeria practitioner will live harmoniously in nature with the Orishas.

TABLE OF CONTENTS

1

HERBS OF
THE ORISHAS

The herbs (Ewe) of the Orishas (gods) is the glue which binds the healing powers of the earth to the heavens above. Without the sacred ewe it would be impossible for Santeros (Priests of the Santeria Religion) to heal or to invoke the supernatural powers of the Orishas. Each Orisha has specific herbs that are attributed to them. Each herb found in nature represents a path of power established by Olodumare (God the Father). Herbs are used by participants in all of the major initiations, sacred rituals, ceremonies and in magical spells. A Santero Priest is an expert herbalist and knows the secrets and magical powers to a wide variety of herbs. By using their knowledge and expertise in herbalism, a Santero can heal and perform sacred rituals to bring about a positive change. The following is a list of some of the most commonly used herbs and the Orishas associated with them. Although some of the herbs listed are rare and have been taken from traditional historical texts, most are available from any botanica.

ORISHA ELEGGUA

The *Orisha Eleggua* is the *Divine Messenger* of all the other Orishas. Orisha Eleggua is the keeper of the crossroads. It is through the Orisha Eleggua that all magic begins and ends. Herbs associated with the Orisha Eleggua are used for *protection and to open the roads of opportunity and success.* The following are herbs attributed to the Orisha Eleggua.

HERBS

Abre Camino
Alacracillo
Arrasa,
Aji Picante
Almacigo
  de Cuartro Caminos
Aguimuldo
Ateji
All Spice
Anis
Angelica
Asofoetida
Boton De Oro
Barriguilla
Belo
Basil
Bergamot Mint
Balm of Gilead
Cascara De Coco
Manteca De Corojo
Cafe
Camphor
Clove
Copal
Cumin
Cayenne Pepper
Calamas
Dragon's Blood
Dill
Espartillo
Eucalyptus

Grains of Paradise
Guayaba
Guaro
Gandules
Guncalote
Geranium
Garlic
Gardenia
Ginger
Hortiguilla
Hedionda
Hierba Mentirosa
Hojos del Frijol
  de Carita
Hojas De Aguacate
Hisbiscus
Heliotrope
Horehound
Heather
Honey Suckle
Hyacinth
Hyssop
Itamo Real
Juniper
Lengua De Vaca
Llamao
Lemon Balm
Lime
Lavander
Lilac
Lotus

Menta
Mausfuerzo
Malojo
Meloncillo
Meadow Sweet
Mallow
Myrrh
Marigold
Mandrake
Mistletoe
Mugwort
Mimosa
Orille
Orange
Orris
Pica Pica
Pendejera
Pinon Blanca
Pata de Gallina
Pinga Hermosa
Pinon Criollo
Pastillo
Peppermint
Pine
Petitgrain
Rabo de Zorra
Rosemary
Rue
Raiz de Aquncaté,
Rose Geranium
Salt Peter

Salguso
Sage
Sandlewood
Snap Dragon
Travesura
Tallo de Maiz

Thistle
Varica
Vente Comigo
Vertiver
Violet
Valeriana

Vervain
Wormwood
Yerba Fina
Yarrow

ORISHA OBATALA

The *Orisha Obatala* is known as the *Father of Purity and Light*. The Orisha Obatala is associated with *spiritual healing and cleansing ceremonies*. Herbs associated with Orisha Obatala are generally used for healing and protection. The following are herbs attributed to the Orisha Obatala.

HERBS

Algadon
Almond
Aguinaldo Blanco
Angelica
All Spice
Bleo Blanco
Basil
Bay
Campana Blanca
Calamas
Carnation
Cedarmood
Citron,
Clove
Copal
Cumin
Canutillo Blanco,
Coriander
Drangon's Blood
Eguere Tete
Eucalyptus

Frankincense
Ferns
Fennel
Flor De Agua (White)
Guanabana
Garlic
Gardenia
Galangal
Geranium
Huiguereta
Heliotrope
Horehound
Honeysuckle
Heather
Hyssop
Jagua Blanco
Lilacs (White)
Lime
Lemon Balm,
Lavender
Lotus

Mata De Pincho
Malva
Mallow
Myrrh
Mistletoe
Mugwort
Mandrake
Marigold
Orris
Peregun
Prodigiosa
Peoria
Peppermint
Pine
Patchouly
Penny Royal
Peony
Petitgrain
Roses (White)
Rose Geranium
Rue

Sanco Blanco	Thistle	Vetivert
San Diego	Thyme	Valeriana
Sage	Vergolaga	Wisteria
Sandalwood (White)	Violet	Yarrow
Snap Dragon	Vervain	

ORISHA CHANGO

The *Orisha Chango* is known in the Santeria religion as the *God of Thunder, Lightening, Power and War.* Herbs associated with the Orisha Chango are usually used to *overcome enemies and self protection.* The following is a list of herbs attributed to the Orisha Chango.

HERBS

Alamo	Carnation	Lilac
Almacigo	Cedar Wood	Lime
Ajo De Goma	Cypress	Lotus
Amansa Guapo	Cumin	Lavender
Artemisas	Dragon's Blood	Mandrake
Ajo Vegetal	Deer's Tongue	Marigold
All Spice	Dell	Minosa
Apricot	Frankincense	Mistletoe
Apple Blossom	Granada	Myrrh
Ambergris	Guayacan	Mamey
Angelica	Geranium	Manzana
Anis	Ginger	Moco De Pavo
Asofoetida	Ginseng	Paraiso
Black Pepper	Grains of Paradise	Pitalla
Basil	Galangal	Plantano
Balm Of Gilead	Huevo De Toro	Pino
Bay Leaves	Heather	Palma Real
Bergumot Mint	Honeysuckle	Palo Bomba
Bledo Punzo	Hyacinth	Pino De Botija
Canutillo Rojo	Hyssop	Patchouly
Camomile	Hisbiscus	Penny Royal
Caraway	Jobo	Peppermint
Clove	Juniper	Pine

Rue	Saffron	Vanilla
Rompe Zaraguey	Sesame	Valeriana
Santa Barbara	Spehanotis	Vervain
Saluadera	Trepadera	Violet
Siguaraya	Tuatua	Yerba Mate
Sage	Thistle	Zarzaparilla
Sandlewood	Tuberose	
Sweet Pea	Vacabuey	

ORISHA OCHUN

The *Orisha Ochun* is the *Goddess Venus* of the Santéria religion. Herbs associated with the Orisha Ochun are generally used to attract love, money and wealth. The following is a list of herbs attributed to the Orisha Ochun.

HERBS

Alambrilla	Cerraja	Galangal, Hierba
Apple Blossom	Culantrilla	Anil
Apricot	Copal	Hierba Buena
All Spice	Coriander	Hierba De La Nina
Almond	Cumin	Hierba Fina
Ambar	Calamus	Hojas de Naranja
Anis	Cedar Wood	Huevo de Gallo,
Achivata	Cinquefoil	Helencho
Ambergris	Clover	Hyacinth
Arabito	Diez del Dia	Hisbiscus
Boton De Oro	Dill	Hazel
Basil	Dragon's Blood	Heather
Berro	Deer's Tongue	Heliotrope
Colonia	Elder	Honey Suckle
Cucaracha	Flor De Agua (Yellow)	Hyssop
Catnip	Feligrama	Irish Moss
Camomile	Fresura	Jasmin
Chick Weed	Guasimo	Lemon Grass
Cinnamon	Grains Of Paradise	Lavender
Civet	Ginger	Lechuga
Clove	Ginseng	Llanten

Lino de Mar	Orasun	Stephanotis
Maravilla	Orris	Sweet Pea
Mazorquilla	Orchid	Sesame Seed
Marilope	Paraquita Morada	Saffron
Mastuerzo	Panetela	St. John's Wort
Majoram	Palo Dulce	Tuberose
Meadow Sweet	Palo de Brazil	Tonka Beans
Myrtle	Palchouly	Uva Morada
Nettle	Parsely	Verbena
Nutmeg	Peppermint	Vanilla
Olive	Plumeria	Yarrow
Orange	Roses (Yellow)	Zarzaprilla
Oak Moss	Rosemary	

ORISHA YEMAYA

The Orisha Yemaya is the Great Mother of the World. The Orisha Yemaya is the Goddess of the Seven Seas. Herbs associated with the Orisha Yemaya are generally used for peace, fertility, protection and to bring calmness to an individual. The following is a list of herbs arrtibuted to the Orisha Yemaya.

HERBS

Anil	Coconut	Hierba Florida
Anamu	Camphor	Jasmin
Algas Marinas	Cumin	Juncos del Mar,
Albahaca Morada	Carnation	Lechuga
Aji	Citron	Lemon
All Spice	Chinzosa	Lotus
Angelica	Eucalyptus	Myrrh
Almond	Esponja	Mugwort
Asofoetida	Flor del Mar	Majagua
Balm of Gilead	Gardenia	Magnolia
Basil	Grape	Meadow Sweet
Berro	Grains of Paradise	Narcissus
Chayote	Grama de la Playa,	Penny Royal
Calamas	Helencho	Peony

Pine	Sandalwood,	Vertivert
Paló Duke	Tuberose	Watermelon
Poppy Seed	Valeriana	

ORISHA OKO

The *Orisha Oko* is associated with *agriculture, fall harvest and the fertility of the land.* Herbs associated with Orisha Oko are generally used by men for fertility and spiritual cleansings. The following is a list of herbs attributed to the Orisha Oko.

HERBS

All grains and vegetables.

All Spice	Coconut	Jasmine
Apricot	Clove	Lemon
Ambergris	Camphor	Myrtle
Almond	Crocus	Magnolia
Angelica	Calamas	Marigold
Anis	Deer's Tongue	Myrrh
Asofoetida	Daisy	Nettle
Bistort	Ginger	Peppermint
Black Pepper	Ginseng	Poppy Seed
Basil	Grains of Paradise	Rosemary
Bergumot Mint	Galangal	Sandlewood
Bay Leaves	Geranium	Tabacco
Coriander	Heather	Tuberose
Cumin	Hyacinth	Willow
Corn	Iris	

ORISHA OLOCUN

The *Orisha Olocun* is associated with the mysteries of the deep oceans. Herbs associated with the Orisha Olocun are generally used to *bring stability and success to an individual.* The following is a list of herbs attributed to the Orisha Olocun.

HERBS

Anil	*Cumin*	*Lechuga*
Anamu	*Camphor*	*Majagua*
Alga Marina	*Coconut*	*Magnolia*
Albahaca	*Caraway Crocus*	*Myrtle*
Aji	*Dragon's Blood*	*Myrrh*
All Spice	*Esponja*	*Mandrake*
Angelica	*Elder*	*Peppermint*
Anis	*Flor del Mar*	*Poppy Seed*
Apple Blossom	*Helencho*	*Palo Duke*
Almond	*Hierbá Buena,*	*Sandlewood*
Bergumot Mint	*Hierba Florida*	*Stephanotis*
Bay Leave	*Jasmin*	*Spearmint*
Berro	*Juncos del Mar*	*Thyme*
Chayoté	*Lotus*	*Tuberose*
Chinzosa	*Lavender*	*Willow*
Calamus	*Lemon Grass*	*Watermelon*
Camomile	*Lemon Verbena*	

ORISHA BABALU-AYE

The *Orisha Babalu-Aye* is known in the Santeria religion as the *Great Healer of Disease and Sickness.* Herbs associated with Orisha Babalu-Aye are generally used for healing. The following is a list of herbs attributed to the Orisha Babalu-Aye.

HERBS

All grains and vegetables.

Apazote	*Alacrancilla*	*Ajonjoli*
Ajeje	*Angariya*	*Angelica*

All Spice	Eucalyptus	Myrrh
Acacia	Ferns	Mistletoe
Almond	Frankincense	Mugwort
Anis	Fennel	Olivo
Asofoetida	Frijoles	Orris
Basil	Guagusi	Pica Pica
Bay Leaves	Gardenia	Palmarosa
Balm of Gilead	Ginger	Poppy Seed
Bergumont Mint	Garlic	Peppermint
Cundiamor	Hierba Nina	Rosa De Jerico
Casimon	Hierba Vieja	Retamo
Campana Morada	Habey	Rosemary
Copal	Heneguey	Rue
Clove	Heliotrope	Sandlewood
Cumin	Honeysuckle	Salvia
Cedar Wood	Hyssop	Tenguetengue
Calamas	Hyacinth	Tapa Camino
Carnation	Jayabico	Tuna
Citron	Juniper	Thyme
Cinnamon	Lime	Tuberose
Coriander	Lotus	Yalla
Clover	Lavender	Yarrow
Cypress	Llamgua	Zaragoza
Camphor	Mani	Zazafran
Escoba Amargo	Mariposa	

ORISHA ORUNLA

The *Orisha Orunla* is known in the Santeria religion as the *Great Diviner of Prophecy*. Herbs associated with the Orisha Orunla are generally associated with *clarity of mind and the powers of spiritual communication.* The following is a list of herbs attributed to the Orisha Orunla.

HERBS

Anis	Chincita	Cinquefoil
All Spice	Cinnamon	Coconut
Baston De Orunla	Carnation	Calamas

Citron	Guanina	Malambre
Camphor	Heliotrophe	Mimosa
Cope	Honeysuckle	Orris
Colozo	Jasmine	Para Mi
Dittany of Crete	Lilac	Pendijeva,
Dragon's Blood	Lemon Grass	Sandlewood
Ginger	Maiz	Sage
Galan De Noche	Mirto	Uvancillo
Guasimito	Marigold	Worm Wood
Gengibre	Madreselva	Wisteriá

ORISHA OYA

The *Orisha Oya* is the *Goddess of the Winds and the Cemetery Gates*. Herbs associated with the Orisha Oya are generally *associated with spiritual cleansings as well as destruction*. Herbs associated with the Orisha Oya are also used to *bring an individual supernatural power*. The following is a list of herbs attributed to the Orisha Oya.

HERBS

Alcanfor	Dittany of Crete	Myrrh
Artimisa	Espanta Muerto	Nutmeg
Anis	Espanta Policia	Oakmoss
Bonita	Flor del Cementerio	Palo Caja
Cinnamon	Flamboyan	Poplar
Carnation	Guaro	Quita Maldicion
Calamus	Geranio	Star Anis
Ciruela	Hibiscus	Sandlewood
Cambia Voz	Lemon	Tangerine
Cabo De Haca	Lime	Varia
Clove	Llanten	Vergonzosa
Camitillo	Mazorguilla	Yucca
Dragon's Blood	Maravilla	Zazaparilla

ORISHA OCHOSI

The *Orisha Ochosi* is known as the *Great Hunter and Protector* of the Santeria religion. Herbs associated wilh the Orisha Ochosi are generally used for *protection and to fight legal matters.* The following is a list of herbs attributed to the Orisha Ochosi.

HERBS

Albahaca Morada	Dragon's Blood	Nettle
All Spice	Espartilla	Pata De Gallina
Asofoetida	Espantá Policia	Parral
Anamu	Ebana	Palo Manaju
Amansa Guapo	Espanta Muerto	Pegojo
Anis	Galangal	Quita Maldicion
Basil	Ginger	Rosemary
Broom	Hueso de Gallo	Salvadera
Cinquefoil	Hyssop	Siempre Viva
Coriander	Honeysuckle	Tabacco
Cumin	Higuerta	Worm Wood
Clove	Incienso Guineo	Woodruff
Cercelera	Jia Blanca	Yerba Mora
Cana Santa	Mistletoe	Yerba DeSangre
Deer's Tongue	Maple	

ORISHA OGGUN

The *Orisha Oggun protects individuals from tragedies and accidents.*The Orisha Oggun is also *associated with policemen, soldiers, physicians and welders.* Herbs associated wilh the Orisha Oggun are generally used for protection. The following is a list of herbs attributed to the Orisha Oggun.

HERBS

Anamu	Angelica	Basil
Adormidera	Anis	Bay
Amansa Guapo	Asofoetida	Bergumot Mint
Almasigo	Bibijagua	Cana Santa

11

Capana Morada	Hyacinth	Pica De Gato
Clove	Hyssop	Pigoja
Cypress	Honeysuckle	Peony
Cumin	Jiqui	Petitgrain
Carnation	Juniper	Palchouly
Caraway	Lotus	Quita Maldicion
Copal	Lime	Rosemary
Dragon's Blood	Lilac	Rompe Zaraguey
Escandon	Mandrake	Roses
Ebana	Misiletoe	Rabo De Piedra
Eucalyptus	Minosa	Siempre Viva
Galangal	Mugwort	Salvadera
Guanabana	Myrrh	Una de Gato
Guao	Orris	Violet
Hierba Florida	Pimienta Roja	Vervain
Higuerta	Pimienta Negra	Vetivert
Hoja De Roble	Palo Manaju	Yerba de Sangre
Hueso De Gallo	Palo Bomba	Zazaparilla
Heather		

ORISHA OZAIN

The *Orisha Ozain* is the owner of all herbs that exists on earth. The Orisha Ozain *controls the forces of nature and knows all of the secret magical usages to every herb.* Herbs associated with Orisha Ozain will *bring an individual protection, supernatural power and communication with the spirits.* The most important herbs attributed to Orisha Ozain are found in dense forest and high mountainous regions. The most sacred of these herbs are called *palos* (tree sticks) which are used in the magical spells by Priests of the Palo Mayombe religion. The Orisha Ozain is one of the most important deities venerated by Paleros. A Palero Priest who is well versed in the secrets of herbal magic is often times called Ozainista.

PALOS

A Palero Priest is also an expert herbalist as well as a powerful magician. One of the greatest and powerful tools that a Palero can use is the Palo. Palos as termed in Spanish are special tree sticks that are used extensively in the practice of Palo Mayombe. These magical tree sticks when used in the correct way will produce great supernatural power. Each palo is attributed to a specific Orisha or spirit and has its own unique magical purpose. There are many different ways that palos can be used in magical ceremonies, rituals and in the making of supplies used in the Santeria and Palo Mayombe religions. Before making any products, it is necessary to familarize yourself with their names and magical usages. The following are the most popular palos used in magical spells and spiritual offerings for the Orishas and the spirits of Palo Mayombe.

Palo Mullato - This palo is associated with *Orisha Chango* and *Orisha Ozain*. This palo is used to dominate or to bewitch an individual.

Palo Mullato - This palo is associated with the Orisha Oya. This palo is used to change a person's luck to the worse.

Palo Mullato - This extremely rare palo is associated with the Orisha Eleggua and Orisha Chango. This palo is used to remove negative obstacles from an individuals path.

Palo Bomba - This palo is associated with the Orisha Chango, Oriska Oggun and Orisha Oya. This palo is used to destroy the foundation of an individual.

Palo Cabalerro - This palo is associated with the Orisha Eleggua, OrishaYemaya and Orisha Ochosi. This palo is used to reverse wilhccraft and in spiritual cleansings.

Palo Cambia Voz - This palo is associated with the Orisha Ochun and Orisha Ozain. This palo is used to change an individual's opinion.

Palo Caja - This palo is associated with the Orisha Oya, Orisha Oggun, Orisha Ochosi and Orisha Chango. This palo is used to punish or destroy a witch

Palo Guaramo - This palo is associated with the Orisha Eleggua, Orisha Obutala and Orisha Ochosi. This palo is used for protection and inside amulets.

Palo Guama - This palo is associated with the spirit Zarabanda and the Spirit Lucero. This palo is used to open up the gates of hell and to the realm of the spirits.

Palo Cocuyo - This palo is associated with the Orisha Ozain. This palo is used to control the forces of nature.

Palo Espuelde Gallo - This palo is associated with the Orisha Eleggua, Orisha Ochosi and Orisha Oggun. This palo is used to shut a person's mouth.

Palo Santo - This palo is associated with the Orisha Oggun, Orisha Oya and Orisha Chango. This palo is used to shut a person's eyes.

Palo Tocino - This palo is associated with the Orisha Eleggua, Orisha Chango, Orisha Oya and Orisha Ozain. This palo is used to kill a witch.

Palo Amargo - This palo is associated with the Orisha Chango and OrishaYemaya. This palo is used for protection and victory over enemies.

Palo Vence Batalla - This palo is associated with the Orisha Chango and the spirit of the Prenda Judia.

Palo Jina - This palo is associated with the Orisha Yemaya, Orisha Chango, Orisha Ochosi and Orisha Oggun. This palo is used in amulets of protection.

Palo Namo - This palo is associated with the Orisha Eleggua. This palo is used to open the roads to opportunity and success.

Palo Dulce - This palo is associated with the OrishaYemaya and Orisha Ochun. This palo Is used In love and domination spells.

Palo Hueso - This palo is associated with the Orisha Eleggua and Orisha Ochun. This palo is used in money and prosperity spells.

Palo Guayaba - This palo is associated with the Orisha Eleggua, Orisha Ozain and Orisha Chango. This palo is used in spells of Divine Justice and revenge.

Palo Pino - This palo is associated with the Orisha Ozain, Orisha Chango and Orisha Oya. This palo is used in spells of Divine Justice and destruction.

Palo Amansa Guapo - This palo is associated with the Orisha Yemaya, Orisha Ochun and Orisha Chango. This palo is used in love and domination spells.

Palo Jobovan - This palo is associated with the Orisha Eleggua, Orisha Ochosi and Orisha Oggun. This palo is used in court spells and to free an individual from jail.

Palo Canpeche - This palo is associated with the Orisha Eleggua and Orisha Chango. This palo is used to reverse any type of magical spell.

Palo Ojancho - This palo is associated with the Orisha Eleggua, Orisha Chango and Orisha Ochun. This palo is used to cause conflicts and to separate individuals.

Palo Clavo - This palo is associated with Orisha Eleggua and Orisha Oggun. This palo is used to remove a curse or the evil eye.

Palo Jeringa - This palo is associated with the Orisha Yemaya, Orisha Chango and Orisha Ochun. This palo is used in strong love spells.

Palo Diablo - This palo is associated with the Orisha Chango, Orisha Oya and Orisha Ozain. This palo is used in extremely powerful spells of black magic.

Palo Justicia - This palo is associated with the Orisha Eleggua, Orisha Ochosi and Orisha Oggun. This palo is used in court spells to bring an individual to justice.

Palo Para Mi - This palo is associated with the Orisha Ochun. This palo is used in love spells.

Palo Ven a Mi - This palo is associated with the Orisha Ochun. This palo is used in love spells to make an individual come to you.

Palo Cambia Rumba - This palo is associated with the Orisha Oya, Orisha Eleggua, Orisha Chango and Orisha Ozain. This palo is used to change an individuals luck or fortune for the worse.

Palo Malambo - This palo is associated with the Orisha Ozain and Orisha Eleggua. This palo is used to multiply the forces of nature and darkness.

Palo Moro - This palo is associated with the Orisha Eleggua, OrishaYemaya Orisha Ochun and Orisha Chango. This palo is used to bring an individual luck and love.

Palo Manga Sayas - This palo is associated with the OrishaYemaya, and Orisha Eleggua. This palo is used to keep a marriage or relationship together.

Palo Jabon - This palo is associated with the Orisha Obutala, Orisha Babalu Aye and Orisha Eleggua. This palo is used in strong spiritual cleansings and for protection.

Palo Guasimo - This palo is associated with the Orisha Eleggua, Orisha Ochosi, Oriska Oggun and Orisha Chango. This palo is used to eliminate gossip and to tie an individual's tongue.

Palo Muerto - This palo is associated with the Orisha Eleggua and Orisha Ozain. This palo is used to bring an end to any situation.

Palo Aceituno - This palo is associated with the Orisha Chango and Orisha Ochun. This palo is used to dominate an individual.

Palo Ramon - This palo is associated with the Orishas Chango and Ozain. This palo is used to communicate and control spirits.

Palo Una de Gato - This palo is associated with the Orisha Ozain and Orisha Chango. This palo is used to bewitch an individual.

Palo Abre Camino - This palo is associated with the Orisha Eleggua. This palo is used to bring success to an individual.

Palo Espanta Muerto - This palo is associated with the Orisha Eleggua, Orisha Obatala, Orisha Yemaya and Orisha Chango. This palo is used to protect an individual from the evil eye.

Palo Espanta Policia - This palo is associted with the Orisha Eleggua, Orisha Oggun and Orisha Ochosi. This palo is used to protect an individual from legal problems.

Palo Ceiba- This palo is associted with the Seven African Powers, Eggun (Ancestor Spirits) and the spirits of Palo Mayombre. This palo is used in spiritual cleansings and to bring about spiritual manifestations.

2

MAGICAL
POWDERS

Polvo De Palo is the spanish name which means powdered sticks. All of the palos mentioned in the previus chapters can be used in powdered form. Thesevariety of different ways. The powder can be made using a simple metal file and grinding the wood into a fine sawdust like material. These powders should be placed into labled jars. Making Plovo De Palo can be a lengthy process, but the magical success of many spells may depend upon this magical powder. Powders can be used alone or mixed together depending upon the desired agenda of the spell. All powders can be empowered by using a candle and reciting the appropriate prayer. Powders can be made with a variety of natural items. There are hundreds of powders which can be created and prepared by a Santero or Palero Priest. The following formulas are for some of the most commonly used powders in magical spells. I have used all of the following powders with much success.

PROTECTION POWDER

This powder is used for protection and for victory over enemies. This powder can be used in candle dressings, amulets or sprinkled at the entrance of your home or business.

INGREDIENTS

1. Powdered Palo Amargo
2. Powdered Palo Jina
3. Powdered Palo Jabon
4. Powdered Palo Canpeche
5. Powdered Palo Guaramo
6. Cascarilla
   (powdered egg shell)
7. Cigar
8. Rum
9. White Candle

PREPARATION

1. Place all of the powdered palos in a large bowl.
2. Add the cascarilla in the bowl.
3. Take a mouthful of rum and spray it directly on the powders.
4. Light a cigar and blow the smoke directly on the powders.
5. Recite a prayer to the Seven African Powers.
6. Light the candle and allow it to burn completely.
7. Mix the ingredients well and place them in a storage jar.

DESTROY AN INDIVIDUAL

This powder is used to destroy an individual or to make them move from their residence. The powder can be sprinkled in the individuals home or place of business. Once the powder has been used, it will only be a matter of days before the problems begin.

INGREDIENTS

1. Powdered Palo Santo
2. Powdered Palo Vence Batalla
3. Powdered Palo Muerto
4. Black Salt
5. Rum
6. Cigar
7. Black Candle

PREPARATION

1. Place all of the powdered palos in a bowl.
2. Add the Black Salt to the bowl.

3. *Take a mouthful of rum and spray it directly on the ingredients.*
4. *Light a cigar and blow the smoke directly on the ingredients.*
5. *Recite a prayer to the Seven Intranquil Spirits.*
6. *Light the candle and allow it to completly burn.*
7. *Mix the ingredients well and place them in a storage jar.*

If this powder is sprinkled into the yard or lawn of an individual, they will never be able to get rid of the problems unless they move from that residence or business location.

SEPARATION POWDER

This powder is used to separate or cause conflict between individuals This powder can be sprinkled inside the individual's home.

INGREDIENTS

1. *Powdered Palo Muerto*
2. *Powdered Palo Diablo*
3. *Powdered Palo Ojancho*
4. *Rum*
5. *Cigar*
6. *Four Red Candles*
7. *Cascarilla*
   (powdered eggshell)

PREPARATION

1. *Place all of the powdered palos in a bowl.*
2. *Draw the circle of the spirit Zarabanda and place the bowl in the center.*
3. *Take a mouthful of rum and spray it directly on the ingredients.*
4. *Light the cigar and blow the smoke directly on the ingredients.*
5. *Place the candles around the circle and then light.*
6. *Recite the prayer of the spirit Zarabanda and allow the candles to burn completely.*
7. *Place the powder in a storage jar.*

If your spouse or lover is having an affair, simply sprinkle same of this powder into their clothes before they leave to see the other person. This powder can also be sprinkled in front of the other persons house.

BEWITCHING POWDER

This powder is used to bewitch an individual or location. The powder can be sprinkled or transfered to others by shaking their hands.

INGREDIENTS

1. Powdered Palo Una De Gato
2. Powdered Palo Aceituno
3. Powdered Scorpion
4. Rum
5. Cigar
6. Black Candle

PREPARATION

1. Place all of the powdered palos in a bowl.
2. Add the powdered scorpion to the bowl.
3. Take a mouthful of ram and spray it directly on the ingredients.
4. Light the cigar and blow the smoke directly on the ingredients.
5. Recite a prayer to the Intranquil Spirits and then light the candle.
6. Allow the candle to burn completely.
7. Place the powder in a storage jar.

LOVE POWDER

This is an extremely powerful powder used in love spells. The powder when properly made will make an individual fall instantly in love with you. The powder can be sprinkled in the individuals home or used in perfumes. This powder can be used by both men and women.

INGREDIENTS

1. Powdered Palo Dulce
2. Powdered Palo Una De Gato
3. Powdered Palo Amansa Guapo
4. Powdered Palo Santo
5. Powdered Cinnamon
6. Rum
7. Cigar
8. Seven African Powers Candle
   (7 day glass candle)

PREPARATION

1. Place all of the powdered palos in a bowl.
2. Add the powdered cinnamon to the bowl.

3. *Take a mouthful of rum and spray it directly on the ingredients.*
4. *Light the cigar and blow the smoke directly on the ingredients.*
5. *Recite a prayer to the Seven African Powers and light the candle.*
6. *Allow the candle to burn completely.*
7. *After the seven days, place the powder in a storage jar.*

PROSPERITY POWDER

This powder is used to bring money and luck in gambling. The powder can be used in amulets or rubbed on the hands before playing a game of chance.

INGREDIENTS

1. *Powdered Palo Namo*
2. *Powdered Palo Hueso*
3. *Cascarilla (eggshell powder)*
4. *Holy Water*
5. *Rum*
6. *Cigar*
7. *Seven African Powers Candle (7 day religious candle)*

PREPARATION

1. *Place all of the powdered palos in a bowl.*
2. *Add the Cascarilla powder to the bowl.*
3. *Take a mouthful of rum and spray it directly on the ingredients.*
4. *Light the cigar and blow the smoke directly on the ingredients.*
5. *Sprinkle a small amount of Holy Water over the ingredients.*
6. *Light the candle and recite a prayer to the Seven African Powers.*
7. *Allow the candle to burn completely.*
8. *After seven days, place the powder in a storage jar until ready to use.*

COURT VICTORY POWDER

This powder can be used to win a court or legal battle. This extremely powerful powder can be sprinkled in front of the court house on the day of court. For the best results, sprinkle a little of this powder on the court room floor. When the powder hits the floor, the courtroom will be under the control of powerful spirits that will assist you in a victory.

INGREDIENTS

1. Powdered Palo Camito
2. Powdered Palo Santo
3. Powdered Palo Espuelde Gallo
4. Powdered Palo Cambia Voz
5. Powdered Palo Guayaba
6. Powdered Palo Jobovan

7. Polvo De Venado
   (powdered deer horn)
8. Cascarilla (eggshell powder)
9. 25 Red Candles
10. Rum
11. Cigar

PREPARATION

1. Place all of powdered palos in a bowl.
2. Add the Polvo De Venado to the bowl.
3. Using the cascarilla, draw the circle of the spirit Zarabanda on the ground and place the bowl in the center.
4. Take a mouthful of rum and spray it directly on the ingredients.
5. Light the cigar and blow the smoke directly on the ingredients.
6. Place five candle around the bowl and light. Allow the candles to burn completely.
7. Do this for five consecutive days. The powder is ready to use after the fifth day.

SCORPION POWDER

Powdered scorpions are used in spells of domination and protection. This powder can be sprinkled over the name or picture of an individual to dominate or to cause them problems.

INGREDIENTS

1. Powdered Palo Aceituno
2. Powdered Palo Amargo

3. Scorpion
4. Four Red Candles

PREPARATION

1. Take a dried scorpion and pulverize it into a fine powder
2. Place the scorpion powder in a bowl.
3. Place all of the powdered palos in the bowl.
4. Place the candles around the bowl and light.
5. Recite a prayer to the Orisha Chango.
6. Allow the candles to complelly burn.
7. Place the powder in a storage jar.

POWDER OF THE DEAD

The powder of the dead is used in spells and rituals common in the practice of Voodoo and Palo Mayombe. The powder is used when you need to send mischevious spirits to perform a deed or task.

INGREDIENTS

1. Powdered Palo Ramon
2. Powdered Palo Cocuyo
3. Powdered Palo Mulato
4. Powdered Palo Diablo
5. Powdered Hueso De Muerto
   (powdered human bone)
6. Red Chile Powder
7. Black Pepper
8. Three Pennies
9. Black Candle
10. Black Cloth 9 in. x 9 in.

PREPARATION

1. Place all of the powdered palos in a bowl.
2. Add the Hueso de Muerto red chile pepper and black pepper to the bowl.
3. Recite a prayer to the Intranquil Spirits and mix well.
4. Bundle all of the ingredients up in the black cloth with the three pennies
5. Bury the bundle over a grave and place the candle in the center of the dirt mound.
6. Light the candle and leave buried for nine nights.
7. Remove after nine days and place the powder in a storage jar until ready to use.

POWDER OF THE WARRIORS

This powder is called in Spanish, Polvo De Los Guerreros. A very rare magic powder that is extracted from the cauldron of the Orisha Oggun and Ochosi. This powder is used to overcome enemies and in amulets of protection.

INGREDIENTS

1. Cauldron of the Orisha Oggun
   (consecrated)
2. White Candle
3. Rum
4. Cigar

PREPARATION

1. *Light the candle and place it next to the cauldron.*
2. *Recite a prayer to Oriska Oggun and the Orisha Ochosi.*
3. *Take a mouthful of rum and spray it directly on the implements of Orisha Oggun and Orisha Ochosi.*
4. *Light the cigar and blow the smoke directly in the cauldron.*
5. *Scrape the bottom of the cauldron.*
6. *Place the powder in a storage jar until ready to use.*

GANGA POWDER
(Original Polvo De Prenda)

This very powerful powder is used to conjure the spirits of the dead. This is the all purpose destruction powder. The powder is scraped from the bottom of the spiritual cauldron of the spirit Zarabanda.

INGREDIENTS

1. *Cauldron of Zarabanda (consecrated)*
2. *Rum*
3. *Cigar*
4. *Red Candle*

PREPARATION

1. *Light the candle and place it next to the cauldron of Zarabanda.*
2. *Recite the prayer of Zarabanda.*
3. *Take a mouthful of rum and spray it directly on the spirit.*
4. *Light the cigar and blow the smoke directly in the cauldron of Zarabanda.*
5. *Salute the spirit in the cauldron and ask for permission to retrieve some of the sacred powder.*
6. *Scrape the edges of the cauldron.*
7. *Place the powder in a dark storage jar until ready to use.*

POWDERED AFRICAN FROG

Powdered African Frog is used in magical spells to dominate or make an individual sick. The powder is is placed over pictures or placed in the stomachs of voodoo dolls. A very fast acting magical ingredient.

INGREDIENTS

1. Dried African Frog
2. Powdered Palo Pino
3. Powdered Palo Muerto
4. Red Candle

PREPARATION

1. Using a metal file, pulverize the dried African Frog.
2. Place the powdered African Frog in a bowl.
3. Add all of the powdered palos in the bowl.
4. Recite a prayer to the spirits of the forest.
5. Light the candle and allow it to burn completly.
6. Place the powder in a storage jar until ready to use.

DEERHORN POWDER

Deerhorn powder (Polvo De Venado) is used in spells of the Orisha Ochosi. This powder is used to release an individual from jail or to win a court battle. Sprinkle this powder on the courtroom floor on the day of the trial.

INGREDIENTS

1. Deerhorns
2. Anisette Liquor
3. White Candle
   (seven day religious candle)

PREPARATION

1. Take a piece of deers horn and place it in a bowl.
2. Pour the Anisette Liquor over the horn.
3. Recite a prayer to the Orisha Ochosi and light the candle.
4. Allow the deerhorn to remain in the Anisette Liquor for seven days.
5. On the 8th day, remove the deerhorn and allow it to dry.
6. After the deerhorn has dried, grate it with a file into a fine powder.
7. Place the powder in a storage jar until ready to use.

SPIRIT POWDER

This powder is used by Palero Priests to bring them supernatural powers. This powder is rubbed on the hands before beginning a magical ritual or ceremony.

INGREDIENTS

1. Powdered Palo Aceituno
2. Powdered Palo Canpeche
3. Powdered Palo Guamo
4. Powdered Palo Cocuyo
5. Powdered Palo Santo
6. Powdered Palo Caballero
7. Powdered Palo Diablo
8. Powdered Palo Malambo
9. Powdered Hueso De Muerto (powdered human bone)
10. Nine Black Candles
11. Rum
12. Cigar
13. Cascarilla (powdered eggshell)

PREPARATION

1. Using the cascarilla, draw the circle of the spirit Zarabanda.
2. Place all of the powdered palos in a bowl and place it in the center.
3. Place the nine candles around the bowl.
4. Take a mouthful of rum and spray it directly on the ingredients.
5. Light the cigar and blow the smoke directly on the ingredients.
6. Recite a prayer to the spirit Zarabanda and light the candles. Allow the candles to burn completly.
7. After the 9th night, remove it and store until ready to use.

POWDER SPIDERS

Powdered spiders are used in love and domination spells. The powder can be used in candle dressings.

INGREDIENTS

1. Dried Poisonous Spiders
2. Powdered Palo Santo
3. Black Candle
4. Red Candle

PREPARATION

1. Pulverize the dried spiders into a fine powder and place them in a bowl.
2. Place the powdered Palo Santo in the bowl.

3. Place the black and red candles next to the bowl and then light.
4. Recite a prayer to summon the spirit of the spider.
5. Allow the candles to burn completely.
6. Place the powder in a dark storage jar until ready to use.

CONFLICT POWDER #1

This powder is used to bring an individual conflicts. It can be used in candle dressings or sprinkled in the individuals home or business location.

INGREDIENTS

1. Black Cat Fur   *4. Cemetery Dirt*
2. Black Dog Fur   *5. Black Candle*
3. Powdered Bat

PREPARATION

1. Burn the hair from the dog and cat into a fine powder.
2. Place the fine powder in a bowl.
3. Add the powdered bat to the bowl.
4. Add the cemetery dirt to the bowl.
5. Mix all of the ingredients well.
6. Recite a prayer to the Intranquil Spirits.
7. Light the candle and allow it to complelly burn.
8. Place the powder in a dark storage jar until ready to use.

CONFLICT POWDER #2

INGREDIENTS

1. Monkey feces   *4. Black Rooster Wing Feathers*
2. Dirt from where two dogs fought *5. Black Candle*
3. Bullhorn Powder

PREPARATION

1. Pulverize the dried monkey feces into a fine powder.
2. Place the powdered monkey feces in a bowl.

3. Add the dirt from where two dogs fought to the bowl.
4. Add the powdered bullhorn to the bowl.
5. Burn the rooster feathers and place the powder in the bowl.
6. Mix the ingredients well.
7. Light the candle and recite a prayer to the Intranquil Spirits.
8. Allow the candles to completely burn.
9. Place the powder in a storage jar until ready to use.

CONFLICT POWDER #3

INGREDIENTS

1. Fighting Cock's Spur
   (from a black rooster leg)
2. Black Salt
3. Wasp Nest

4. Nine Hornets
5. Black Pepper
6. Black Candle

PREPARATION

1. File the fighting cock's spur into a fine powder.
2. Place the powder in a bowl.
3. Add the black salt and black pepper to the bowl.
4. Pulverize the nine hornets and the wasp's nest into a fine powder.
5. Place the powder in the bowl.
6. Mix the ingredients well.
7. Recite a prayer to the Intranquil Spirits and light the candle.
8. Allow the candle to burn completely.
9. Place the powder in a dark storage jar until ready to use.

LOVE POWDER

INGREDIENTS

1. Dried Hummingbird
2. Powdered Palo Amansa Guapo
3. Powdered Ven a Mi
4. Powdered Cinnamon
5. Red Candle

PREPARATION

1. Burn the dried hummingbird into a fine powder.
2. Place the powder in a bowl.
3. Add all of the powdered palos and cinnamon to the bowl.
4. Recite a prayer to the hummingbird and light the candle.
5. All the candle to burn completely.
6. Mix the ingredients well.
7. Place the powder in a storage jar.

SNAKE POWDER

This powerful snake powder is used in love and domination spells.

INGREDIENTS

1. Dried Venomous Snake
2. Powdered Palo Amargo
3. Powdered Palo Santo
4. Red Candle

PREPARATION

1. Pulverize the snake into a fine powder.
2. Place the powder in a bowl.
3. Add all of the powdered palos to the bowl.
4. Recite a prayer to the Intranquil Spirits and then light.
5. Allow the candle to completly burn.
6. Mix the ingredients well.
7. Place the powder in a storage jar until ready to use.

DOVE'S EGG POWDER

Powdered dove's eggs are used in cleansing and protection spells. This powder can be used in the same way as Cascarilla (powdered chicken eggshells).

INGREDIENTS

1. Seven White Dove's Eggs
2. Holy Water

3. White Candle
    (seven day religious candle)

PREPARATION

1. Place the dove's eggs in a bowl.
2. Pour the Holy Water over the eggs .
3. Recite a prayer to the Orisha Obotala and light the candle.
4. Allow the eggs to remain for seven days.
5. After the seven days, remove the yolks and then pulverize the shell.
6. Place the powder in a storage jar until ready to use.

GUINEA HEN EGG POWDER

Powdered Guinea Hen eggs are used in domination and protection spells. The powder can be placed inside the amulets of the Orisha Ozain or the Orisha Ochosi to escape the law or enemies.

INGREDIENTS

1. Seven Guinea Hen Eggs
2. Holy Water

3. Red Candle
    (seven day religious candle)

PREPARATION

1. Place the Guinea Hen's eggs in a bowl.
2. Pour the Holy Water over the eggs.
3. Recite a prayer to the Oriskas Ochosi and Ozain.
4. Light the candle and allow it to completely burn.
5. After the seven days, remove the yolks and then pulverize the shell.
6. Place the powder in a storage jar until ready to use.

POWDERED LORO AFRICANO EGG

This powder is extremely rare and powerful. This powder will protect an individual from death and tragic accidents. The powder can be sprinkled or placed inside powerful amulets of the Orishas Obutala and Orisha Babalu Aye.

INGREDIENTS

1. Seven Eggs from the African Grey Parrot

2. Holy Water from Seven Churches

3. Coconut Milk

4. White Candle (seven day religious candle)

PREPARATION

1. Pulverize the egg shells into a fine powder.

2. Place the powder in a jar.

3. Add the Holy Water to the jar.

4. Add the coconut milk to the jar.

5. Recite a prayer to the Orishas Obutala and Babalu Aye.

6. Light the candle and allow it to burn completely.

7. Allow the egg shells to remain for seven days.

8. After the seventh day, strain the liquid mixture over cheese cloth .

9. Allow powder to dry and then place in a storage jar until ready to use.

BULL HORN POWDER

This powder is used in spells of protection and domination.

INGREDIENTS

1. Bull Horn

2. Red Candle

3. Cascarilla (eggshell powder)

PREPARATION

1. Using a metal file, grate the bull's horn into a fine powder.

2. Place the powder in a bowl.

3. Add the cascarilla powder to the bowl.

4. Mix the ingredients well.

5. Recite a prayer to the Orisha Chango and light the candle.

6. Allow the candle to burn completely.

7. Place the powder in a storage jar.

JUNGLE POWDER

This is a very rare and powerful powder used in Central American Black Magic. The powder is used in domination spells. This powder is also used to free an individual from jail. This powder can also be sprinkled over the photograph of an individual to make them go crazy.

INGREDIENTS

1. Bone from a Monkey
2. Bone from a Lion
3. Bone from a Leopard
4. Bone from a Deer
5. Bone from a Snake
6. Bone from a Wolf
7. Bone from a Jaguar
8. Seven African Powers Candle
   (14 day religious candle)

PREPARATION

1. Pulverize all of the bones into a fine powders.
2. Place the powders together in a bowl.
3. Light the candle and recite a prayer to the Seven African Powers.
4. Allow the candle to burn completely.
5. Place the powder in a dark storage jar until ready to use.

REVERSE POWDER

This powder is used to reverse the evil eye and in money spells.

INGREDIENTS

1. Deer Eye Seed
2. Brown Mustard Seeds
3. Cascarilla (eggshell powder)
4. Alum (mineral rock)
5. White Candle
   (7 day religious candle)

PREPARATION

1. Pulverize the Deer Eye seed and the Alum into a fine powder.
2. Place the powder in a bowl.
3. Add the mustard seeds to the bowl.
4. Add the cascarilla powder to the bowl.
5. Mix all of the ingredients well.
6. Light the candle and recite a prayer to the Orisha Obutala.
7. Allow the candle to completely burn.
8. Place the powder in a storage jar until ready to use.

ATTRACTION POWDER

This powder is used by a women to attract love and wealt
can be worn on a daily basis

INGREDIENTS

1. *Talisman Powder (white)*
2. *Hair from a Menstruating Dog*
3. *Powdered Abalone Shell*
4. *Deerhorn Powder*
5. *White Precipitate Powder*
   (Spanish mineral powder)
6. *Powdered Cinnamon*

7. *Powdered Pigeon Egg*
8. *Cascarilla (eggshell powde*
9. *Powdered Valerain (herb)*
10. *Powdered Palo Ven a Mi*
11. *Powdered Palo Amansa Gu*
12. *Yellow Candle*
    (7 day religious candle)

PREPARATION

1. *Burn and pulverize the dog's hair into a fine powder.*
2. *Place the dog's hair powder in a bowl.*
3. *Add the powdered abalone shell, deerhorn powder, powd(
   cinnamon, powdered pigeon egg, powdered valerain, powdered ,
   ven a mi, powdered pale amansa guapo and the cascarilla to the b*
4. *Add the talisman powder and the white precipitate powder to the
   bowl.*
5. *Mix all of the ingredients well.*
6. *Light the candle and recite a prayer to the Orisha Ochun.*
7. *Allow the candle to completely burn.*
8. *Place the powder in a storage jar until ready to use.*

GET AWAY POWDER

This powder is used to make an individual stay away. Sprin
the powder where the individual walks on a daily basis.

INGREDIENTS

1. *Cemetery Dirt*
2. *Pica Pica Powder (Spanish herb)*
3. *Dog feces*
4. *Cumin Powder (herb)*

5. *Black Pepper*
6. *Black Candle*
   (7 day religious candle)

PREPARATION

1. *Pulverize the cemetery dirt and the dog feces into a fine powder.*
2. *Place the powder in a bowl.*
3. *Add the pica pica powder to the bowl.*
4. *Add the cumin powder to the bowl.*
5. *Add the black pepper to the bowl.*
6. *Mix all of the ingredients well.*
7. *Light the candle and recite a prayer to the Intranquil Spirits.*
8. *Allow the candle to burn completely.*
9. *Place the powder in a dark storage jar until ready to use.*

HOT FOOT POWDER

This powder is used in domination spells. The powder is placed in the shoes of an individual that you want to bewitch. The shoes are then buried in the cemetery.

INGREDIENTS

1. *Red Chile Pepper Powder*
2. *Pica Pica Powder*
3. *Black Pepper*
4. *High John the Conqueror Root (powdered)*
5. *Precipitado Rojo (Spanish mineral powder)*
6. *Red Candle (7 day religious candle)*

PREPARATION

1. *Place the red chile pepper and the pica pica powder in a bowl.*
2. *Add the black pepper and the powdered High John the Conqueror to the bowl.*
3. *Mix all of the ingredients well.*
4. *Light the candle and recite a prayer to the Orisha Chango.*
5. *Allow the candle to burn completly.*
6. *Place the powder in a storage jar until ready to use.*

BLACK SALT POWDER

Black Salt is used quite frequently in a variety of Santeria and Palo Mayombe spells. Black Salt is used to get rid of your enemies or unwanted individuals. Although there are commercial Black Salts available, the most powerful Black Salt is handmade and prepared in the following manner. This is the original recipe.

INGREDIENTS

1. Oak Wood   *3. Black Candle*
2. Water   *(7 day religious candle)*

PREPARATION

1. Reduce the Oak Wood into ashes .
2. Place one pound of the Oak Wood ashes in a large bowl.
3. Add the water to the bowl .
4. Light the candle and recite a prayer to the Intranquil Spirits.
5. Allow the ashes to remain scaling for seven days.
6. When the candle has burned completly, add the ashes into a large iron cauldron.
7. Heat the mixture in the cauldron and allow the water to evaporate.
8. The black residue left on the bottom of the cauldron is called Black Salt.
9. After the cauldron has cooled, scrape the Black Salt from the bottom and place it in a dark storage jar until ready to use.

ORISHA CHANGO POWDER

This powerful powder is used to dominate an individual and in love spells. The powder is made by mixing six different herbs sacred to the Orisha Chango. Light a red candle in the preparation of this powder.

ORISHA YEMAYA POWDER

This powder is used in fertility and protection spells. The powder is made by mixing seven different powdered herbs sacred to the Orisha Yemaya. Light a blue candle in the preparation of this powder.

ORISHA OZAIN POWDER

This powder brings an individual supernatural and psychic abilities. The powder is made with nine different powdered herbs sacred to the Orisha Ozain. Light a Seven African Powers candle in the preparation of this powder.

ORISHA ELEGGUA POWDER

This powder can be used in candle dressings and spells enlisting the aide of the Oriska Eleggua. The powder is made by combining 21 different powdered herbs sacred to the Orisha Eleggua. Light a white candle in the preparation of this powder.

ORISHA OCHUN POWDER

This powder is used in love spells and inside amulets. The powder is made by mixing five different powdered herbs sacred to the Orisha Ochun. Light a yellow candle in the preparation of this powder.

ORISHA OBATALA POWDER

This powder is used in spiritual cleansings and in spells to remove the evil eye. The powder is made by mixing seven different powdered herbs sacred to the Orisha Obutala. Light a white candle in the preparation of this powder.

LION POWDER

This powdered lion's tooth powder is used in spells and amulets of protection. This powder can be used in amulets of Palo Mayombe as well as in amulets of the Orisha Ochosi. Light a red candle in the preparation of this powder.

3

MAGICAL POTIONS FOR SPECIFIC PURPOSES

PROTECT YOUR HOME FROM ENEMIES

INGREDIENTS

1. 1 cup of Powder For Protection
2. 2 cups of Holy Water
3. 1 cup of Coconut Milk
4. 1 tablespoon Coconut Oil
5. 2 Clear Glass Drinking Glasses
6. 7 Day Glass Reverse Candle

PREPARATION

1. Pour one cup of Holy Water into each of the drinking glasses.
2. Add 1/2 cup of coconut milk to each of the drinking glasses.
3. Place one glass next to the front door and the other at the back door.
4. Pour the coconut oil in the top of the glass reverse candle.
5. Light the candle.
6. Sprinkle the Powder for Protection completely around the outside of your home.
7. After the candle has complelly finished burning, throw the liquid from the glasses into the street, away from your home.
8. Do this ritual once a month.

DESTROY AN INDIVIDUAL

INGREDIENTS

1. 1 cup **Powder To Destroy An Individual**

2. Nine Black Candles (6 inch)

3. Nine Pins

PREPARATION

1. Write the individual's name nine times on a piece of brown paper.

2. Insert the nine pins through the paper.

3. Place the paper on a plate.

4. Sprinkle the **Powder To Destroy An Individual** over the paper.

5. Place one black candle in the center of the plate.

6. Light the candle and allow it to completly burn.

7. As the candle is burning say: As this candle burns, so may **name of the individual** also burn.

8. Do this for nine consecutive nights.

9. After the 9th candle has completly burned, burn the piece of paper and mix the ashes with the powder.

10. Sprinkle the powder on the individuals property.

This spell should be performed at 12:00 Midnight.

MAKE AN INDIVIDUAL MOVE

INGREDIENTS

1. 2 tablespoons **Powder to Destroy An Individual**

2. 1/4 cup Urine

3. 1/4 cup White Vineger

1 tblsp. Red Precipitate Powder

PREPARATION

1. Write the individuals name nine times on a piece of brown paper.

2. Insert the paper into a glass bottle.

3. Add the **Powder to Destroy An Individual** to the bottle.

4. Add the Urine to the Bottle.

5. Add the Vineger to the bottle.

6. Add the Precipitate Powder to the bottle.

7. Place the cap tightly on the bottle and shake.

8. Smash the bottle near the front door of the individual's home or business.

TO SEPARATE FRIENDS OR LOVERS

INGREDIENTS

1. *1 tablespoon Cat Fur*
2. *1 tablespoon Dog Fur*

3. *2 tblsp. Separation Powder*

PREPARATION

1. *Write the name of one of the individuals nine times on a piece of brown paper.*
2. *Write the name of the other individual nine times over the over individuals name nine times. The names should cross and intersect in the center.*
3. *Place the paper in the center of a black cloth.*
4. *Sprinkle the Separation Powder over the paper.*
5. *Sprinkle the Dog and Cat fur over the powder.*
6. *Wrap the contents in the black cloth.*
7. *Bury the bundle on the property of the individuals or in the yard of one the individuals.*

TO BEWITCH AN INDIVIDUAL

INGREDIENTS

1. *1 tablespoon Bewitching Powder*
2. *1 cup Red Wine*
3. *1 cup White Vineger*
4. *1 tablespoon Dirt From The Individuals Yard*

5. *1 tablespoon Black Precipitate Powder*
6. *One Black Candle (Taper)*
7. *27 Pins*

PREPARATION

1. *Using the photo of the individual, pierce nine pins through each eye and nine pins through the mouth.*
2. *Insert the photo into a glass bottle.*
3. *Add the Bewitching Powder to the bottle.*
4. *Add the Dirt From The Individuals Yard to the bottle.*
5. *Add the wine and the vinegar to the bottle.*
6. *Add the black precipitate powder to the bottle.*

7. *Place the cap on the bottle and say: As I close this bottle, so may* **name of the individual** *keep their eyes and mouth closed.*
8. *Bury the bottle over a grave.*
9. *Light a black candle over the grave.*

If you do not have a photo of the individual, you can substitute a black cloth voodoo doll to represent the individual.

TO MAKE A PERSON
FALL IN LOVE WITH YOU

INGREDIENTS

1. *1 tablespoon of Your Favorite Perfume /Cologne*
2. *Five Fishing Hooks*
3. *1 tablespoon Love Powder*
4. *1/4 Cup Honey*

PREPARATION

1. *Write your name over the individuals photo five times.*
2. *Insert the fishing hooks through the photo.*
3. *Place the photo in the bottom of a glass jar. (face up)*
4. *Sprinkle the* **Love Powder** *over the photo.*
5. *Pour your favorite perfume/cologne over the photo.*
6. *Pour the honey over the photo and seal the jar.*
7. *Place the jar in a dark location where it will not be disturbed or opened.*

TO WIN A LEGAL BATTLE

INGREDIENTS

1. *2 tablespoons Court Victory Powder*
2. *12 Red Candles (6 inch)*

PREPARATION

1. *Write your name across your photo three times. Write your name again in the opposite direction three times.*
2. *Place the photo on a white plate.*

1. Sprinkle the **Court Victory Powder** over the photo.
2. Place four candles around the outer edges of the plate.
3. Light the candles and allow them to completely burn.
4. Do this for three consecutive days before the court hearing.
5. On the day of court, collect the powder from the plate and sprinkle in the front of the court building and the rest inside the court room.

TO WIN AT GAMBLING

INGREDIENTS

1. 2 tablespoons Prosperity Powder   2. Three Green Candles (6 inch)

PREPARATION

1. Write the name of the gambling location three times on a piece of brown paper.
2. Write your name three times across the name of the gambling location. Both names should intersect in the form of a cross.
3. Place the paper on a white plate.
4. Sprinkle the **Prosperity Powder** over the paper.
5. Place one of the candles next to the plate and then light.
6. Recite a prayer to the Seven African Powers and allow the candle to completely burn.
7. Do this for three consecutive days before you will gamble at that location.
8. After the last of the three candles has burned, collect the powder from the plate and sprinkle on the floor of the gambling location.

TO DOMINATE YOUR LOVER

INGREDIENTS

1. 1 tablespoon Scorpion Powder   4. 1/2 cup Snake Oil
2. 1 tablespoon Snake Powder   5. Six Safety Pins
3. 1 tablespoon Cinnamon Powder 6. One Piece of Dirty Clothing
from the desired individual

PREPARATION

1. Write your name across the photo of the desired indivdual six times.
2. Wrap a piece of the individual's clothing around the photo and attach with the six safety pins.
3. Place the wrapped photo at the bottom of a glass jar.
4. Pour the Snake Oil over the photo.
5. Add the **Scorpion Powder** to the jar.
6. Add the Snake Powder and the Cinnamon Powder to the jar.
7. Seal and bury the jar on your property.

PROTECT AN INDIVIDUAL FROM SICKNESS

INGREDIENTS

1. 1 tablespoon Dove's Egg Powder
2. 1 tablespoon Loro Africano Egg Powder
3. 1 tablespoon Cascarilla (Chicken Eggshell Powder)
4. 1 cup Coconut Milk
5. 1 White Chicken Egg
6. White Candle (7 Day Glass Religious)

PREPARATION

1. Mix all of the above ingredients together in a bowl.
2. Recite the Our Father Prayer over the ingredients.
3. Place a photo of the individual on a white plate.
4. Sprinkle the powdered mixture over the photo.
5. Pour the coconut milk over the ingredients.
6. Place the egg in the bowl directly over the photo.
7. Light the candle and allow it to compelly burn.
8. After the candle has finished burning, remove the egg and smash it at an intersection.

4

MAGICAL OILS

Oils have been used for centuries by practioners of magic and the occult. Oils are used to annoint sacred objects, yourself and in magical spells. The following formulas are for the most commonly used spiritual oils used by practioners of the Santeria religion. Making spiritual oils is a simple process and there is a general base formula which can be applied to of the following recipes.

GENERAL OIL FORMULA

- *Add all of essential oils to 1/8 cup of Olive Oil (base oil)*
- *Recite a prayer to the spirit who will empower the oil*
- *Light a corresponding candle*

THE FOLLOWING IS A LIST
OF NATURAL ESSENTIAL OILS

Name	Associated Orisha	Specific Purpose
Acacia	*Orunla*	*Physic awareness, Astral Travel, Spirit Communication*
Almond	*Ochun*	*Money & Wealth*
Allspice	*Seven African Powers*	*Prosperity, Protection, Health*

Name	Associated Orisha	Specific Purpose
Ambergris	*Chango, Oshun*	*Love, Lust*
Ambrosia	*Eleggua*	*Protection from Evil Eye*
Angelica	*Ochosi*	*Protect against Enemies, Legal Matters*
Anise	*Ochosi*	*Court Victories*
Apple	*Chango*	*Love, Domination of Enemies*
Apricot	*Chango, Oshun*	*Love, Marriage*
Aster	*Yemaya, Obatala*	*Peace of MInd*
Azalea	*Oshun*	*Attract Money, Love*
Balsam	*Yemaya*	*Calm a person or situation*
Banana	*Chango*	*Victory*
Bay	*Obatala, Babalu-Aye*	*Healing*
Basil	*Chango*	*Protection, Love*
Bergamot	*Oshun*	*Prosperity, Wealth*
Black Pepper	*Eleggua*	*Destruction, Calamity*
Blue Bonnet	*Eleggua, Oshun*	*Luck to Gamblers*
Calamus	*Ochosi, Oshun*	*Protection, Prosperity*
Camphor	*Elleggua, Ochosi, Oshun*	*Purification rituals, Reverse the Evil Eye*
Carnation	*Babalu-Aye*	*Health , Healing*
Cedar	*Obatala*	*Healing rituals*
Chamomile	*Oshun*	*Love, Money*

Chrysanthimum	Yemaya	Peace, Fertility
Cinnamon	Oshun	Love, Wealth
Civit	Chango	Dominate an individual in love
Clove	Chango	Dominate a lover or bring a lover back
Clover	Oshun	Prosperity in business
Coconut	Eleggua	Success and prosperity to an individual
Coffee	Eleggua	Reverse witchcraft and close the doors of an enemy
Cupress	Yemaya	Peace of mind, tranquility in the home
Dill	Ochosi	Protection, Reunite Lovers
Dragon's Blood	Chango	Reverse the Evil Eye, Banish Evil Spirits
Eucalyptus	Obatala, Babalu-Aye	Fast healing
Evergreen	Ozain	Aphrodisiac for men
Frangipani	Chango, Oshun	Attract love
Frankincense	Orunla	Spiritual communication, Spiritual Cleansing
Gardenia	Obatala	Cleanse an individual's aura, bring clarity of mind
Geranium	Oshun	Attraction, Love

Ginger	*Ozain*	Bring an individual supernatural and magical abilities
Heather	*Eleggua*	Luck and Good Fortune
Helitrope	*Obatala, Orunla*	Healing, psychic awareness
Hemlock	*Ozain*	cause conflict between two people
Hibiscus	*Chango*	Make an individual lustful
Honey	*Oshun*	Love
Hyacinth	*Yemaya*	Peace, Protection, Happiness
Hyssop	*Chango,Ochosi*	Protection
Jasmine	*Orunla*	Prophetic Dreams
Juniper	*Obatala*	Protection, Healing
Lavendar	*Oshun*	Love, Happiness
Lime	*Chango*	Protection
Lemongrass	*Chango, Oshun*	Lust, Love
Lilac	*Oshun, Yemaya*	Bring an individual Peace, Love
Lily	*Obatala, Oshun*	Peace, Tranquility
Lotus	*Oshun*	Love
Magnolia	*Obatala*	Bring an individual peace of mind.
Melon	*Yemaya*	Brings women fertility and blessings

Mistletoe	Ozain	Protection
Musk	Obatala, Oshun	Used by men for protection, also used for purification
Myrrh	Obatala	Protection from the evil eye
Narcissus	Obatala, Yemaya	Peace and tranquility
Nutmeg	Eleggua, Ochosi	Court spells, Open the road to opportunity
Orange	Oshun	Money, Wealth
Orchid	Obatala	Clarity of mind
Orris	Eleggua, Orunla	Psychic awareness
Passion Flower	Chango	Attraction
Patchouly	Chango, Oshun	Love, Domination
Peony	Ochosi	Protection
Peppermint	Ogun, Ochosi, Eleggua	Protection, Psychic Awareness
Pine	Ochosi, Chango	Protection, Money attraction
Pineapple	Chango	Bring back a lover
Rose	Obatala, Yemaya, Oshun	Peace, Healing, Love
Rosemary	Eleggua, Obatala	Healing, Protection from the evil eye
Rue	Eleggua, Obatala	Healing, Protection from witchcraft

Sage	*Eleggua, Obatala*	*Protection from the evil eye, purification*
Sandalwood	*Chango*	*Protection from enemies*
Sassafras	*Oshun*	*Money, Wealth*
Shark	*Olocun*	*Protection, Destroy enemies*
Snake	*Ozain, Chango*	*Dominate individuals*
Spearmint	*Chango, Eleggua*	*Protect your home*
Strawberry	*Chango, Oshun*	*Money, Wealth, Love*
Sweet Pea	*Oshun*	*Attract Love and Money*
Vanilla	*Eleggua*	*Bring good fortune to an individual, home or business*
Vetivert	*Chango, Ogun, Ochosi, Eleggua*	*Chase away evil spirits*
Violet	*Yemaya, Oshun, Obatala*	*Healing, Love, Peace*
Watermelon	*Yemaya*	*Fertility to women, Special requests*
Wintergreen	*Obatala, Babalu Aye*	*Healing*
Wisteria	*Orunla, Obatala*	*Spirituality*
Ylang Ylang	*Eleggua, Oshun*	*Attract love, money, opportunity*

5

OIL FORMULARY

SEVEN AFRICAN POWERS OIL
BASE OIL
7 DROPS ALL SPICE OIL
3 DROPS AMBROSIA OIL
3 DROPS COCONUT OIL
1 DROP PEPPERMINT OIL
SEVEN AFRICAN POWERS CANDLE
PRAYER TO THE
  SEVEN AFRICAN POWERS

ELEGGUA OPPORTUNITY OIL
BASE OIL
7 DROPS COCONUT OIL
3 DROPS NUTMEG OIL
1 DROP HEATHER OIL
WHITE CANDLE
PRAYER TO ORISHA ELEGGUA

ELEGGUA REVERSE OIL
BASE OIL
3 DROPS SPEARMINT OIL
4 DROPS COFFEE OIL
3 DROPS AMBROSIA OIL
BLACK AND RED REVERSE
CANDLE
PRAYER TO ORISHA ELEGGUA

ELEGGUA JOB OIL
BASE OIL
3 DROPS COCONUT OIL
1 DROP ANISE OIL
2 DROPS ORRIS OIL
WHITE CANDLE
PRAYER TO ORISHA ELEGGUA

ELEGGUA MONEY OIL
BASE OIL
7 DROPS COCONUT OIL
1 DROP PEPPERMINT OIL
3 DROPS SASSAFRAS OIL
WHITE CANDLE
PRAYER TO ORISHA ELEGGUA

ELEGGUA DESTRUCTION OIL
BASE OIL
3 DROPS BLACK PEPPER OIL
7 DROPS COFFEE OIL
1 DROP COCONUT OIL
BLACK AND RED REVERSE
CANDLE
PRAYER TO ORISHA ELEGGUA

OBATALA HEALING OIL
BASE OIL
3 DROPS ASTER OIL
1 DROP EUCALYPTUS OIL
3 DROPS COCONUT OIL
3 DROPS SAGE OIL
WHITE CANDLE
PRAYER TO ORISHA OBATALA

OBATALA PEACE OIL
BASE OIL
7 DROPS VIOLET OIL
3 DROPS WISTERIA OIL
4 DROPS COCONUT OIL
WHITE CANDLE
PRAYER TO ORISHA OBUTALA

YEMAYA FERTILITY OIL
BASE OIL
7 DROPS WATERMELON OIL
3 DROPS BALSAM OIL
1 DROP ASTER OIL
BLUE CANDLE
PRAYER TO ORISHA YEMAYA

YEMAYA PROTECTION OIL
BASE OIL
3 DROPS CHRYSANTHMUM OIL
1 DROP LILAC OIL
5 DROPS HYACINTH OIL
BLUE CANDLE
PRAYER TO ORISHA YEMAYA

YEMAYA STABILITY OIL
BASE OIL
7 DROPS COCONUT OIL
3 DROPS ROSE OIL
1 DROP ASTER OIL
BLUE CANDLE
PRAYER TO YEMAYA / OLOCUN

YEMAYA DESTRUCTION OIL
BASE OIL
7 DROPS SHARK OIL
1 DROP CAMPHOR OIL
3 DROPS BLACK PEPPER OIL
BLUE CANDLE
PRAYER TO YEMAYA / OLOCUN

OCHUN LOVE OIL
BASE OIL
3 DROPS AZALEA OIL
2 DROPS AMBERGRIS OIL
5 DROPS CINNAMON OIL
YELLOW CANDLE
PRAYER TO ORISHA OCHUN

OCHUN DOMINATION OIL
BASE OIL
5 DROPS HONEY OIL
2 DROPS LAVENDAR OIL
1 DROP LILAC OIL
1 DROP LOTUS OIL
YELLOW CANDLE
PRAYER TO ORISHA OCHUN

OCHUN MONEY AND GAMBLING OIL
BASE OIL
3 DROPS COCONUT OIL
1 DROP NUTMEG OIL
5 DROPS STRAWBERRY OIL
1 DROP SWEET PEA OIL
YELLOW CANDLE
PRAYER TO ORISHA OCHUN

CHANGO VICTORY OIL
BASE OIL
5 DROPS SANDALWOOD OIL
1 DROP VETIVERT OIL
3 DROPS BANANA OIL
1 DROP APPLE OIL
RED CANDLE
PRAYER TO ORISHA CHANGO

ORISHA CHANGO LOVE OIL
BASE OIL
6 DROPS APRICOT OIL
1 DROP BASIL OIL
1 DROP CLOVE OIL
6 DROPS HISBISCUS OIL
RED CANDLE
PRAYER TO ORISHA CHANGO

CHANGO DOMINATION OIL
BASE OIL
6 DROPS APPLE OIL
1 DROP BANANA OIL
2 DROPS CIVIT OIL
1 DROP HYSSOP OIL
RED CANDLE
PRAYER TO ORISHA CHANGO

OCHOSI COURT VICTORY OIL
BASE OIL
7 DROPS ANGELICA OIL
3 DROPS ANISE OIL
3 DROPS NUTMEG OIL
PURPLE CANDLE
PRAYER TO ORISHA OCHOSI

OCHOSI PROTECTION OIL
BASE OIL
3 DROPS PEONY OIL
5 DROPS PINE OIL
2 DROPS ALL SPICE OIL
PURPLE CANDLE
PRAYER TO ORISHA OCHOSI

OCHOSI ATTRACTION OIL
BASE OIL
1 DROP ALMOND OIL
5 DROPS CINNAMON OIL
1 DROP BLUE BONNET OIL
4 DROPS AMBERGRIS OIL
1 DROP ANISE OIL
PURPLE CANDLE
PRAYER TO ORISHA OCHOSI

OGGUN REVERSE OIL
BASE OIL
3 DROPS ALL SPICE OIL
1 DROP CAMPHOR OIL
3 DROPS VETIVERT OIL
5 DROPS BLACK PEPPER OIL
GREEN CANDLE
PRAYER TO ORISHA OGGUN

OGGUN GET AWAY OIL
BASE OIL
3 DROPS AMBROSIA OIL
2 DROPS ANGELICA OIL
3 DROPS BLACK PEPPER OIL
3 DROPS PEPPERMINT OIL
GREEN CANDLE
PRAYER TO ORISHA OGGUN

BABALU AYE HEALING OIL
BASE OIL
1 DROP SAGE OIL
3 DROPS BAY OIL
1 DROP CEDAR OIL
7 DROPS COCONUT OIL
WHITE CANDLE
PRAYER TO ORISHA BABALU AYE

BABALU AYE PROTECTION FROM EVIL EYE OIL
2 DROPS EUCALYPTUS OIL
3 DROPS LIME OIL
2 DROPS MYRRH OIL
3 DROPS WINTERGREEN OIL
WHITE CANDLE
PRAYER TO ORISHA BABALU AYE

OKO FERTILITY OIL
BASE OIL
3 DROPS ALL SPICE OIL
2 DROPS YANG YLANG
5 DROPS VANILLA OIL
YELLOW CANDLE
PRAYER TO ORISHA OKO

ORUNLA PROPHECY OIL
BASE OIL
3 DROPS COCONUT OIL
1 DROP WISTERIA OIL
3 DROPS JASMIN OIL
3 DROPS FRANKINCENSE OIL
YELLOW AND GREEN CANDLE
PRAYER TO ORISHA ORUNLA

ORUNLA DREAM OIL
BASE OIL
3 DROPS ACACIA OIL
3 DROPS COCONUT OIL
1 DROP MISTLETOE OIL
4 DROPS PEPPERMINT
YELLOW AND GREEN CANDLE
PRAYER TO ORISHA ORUNLA

ORISHA OZAIN SPIRIT OIL
BASE OIL
3 DROPS COCONUT OIL
4 DROPS MISTLETOE OIL
2 DROPS YLANG YLANG OIL
1 DROP PEPPERMINT OIL
SEVEN AFRICAN POWERS CANDLE
PRAYER TO ORISHA OZAIN

OZAIN DIVINATION OIL
BASE OIL
7 DROPS COCONUT OIL
1 DROP ACACIA
1 DROP CAMPHOR OIL
1 DROP EVERGREEN OIL
SEVEN AFRICAN POWERS CANDLE
PRAYER TO ORISHA OZAIN

ZODIAC OILS

AQUARIUS OIL
BASE OIL
3 DROPS PATCHOULY OIL
2 DROPS LAVENDER OIL
1 DROP PEPPERMINT OIL
4 DROPS ACACIA OIL

LIBRA OIL
BASE OIL
3 DROPS ORCHID OIL
1 DROP VANILLA OIL
3 DROPS ROSE OIL
3 DROPS PLUMERIA OIL

ARIES OIL
BASE OIL
3 DROPS CARNATION OIL
4 DROPS JUNIPER OIL
1 DROPS DRAGON'S BLOOD OIL
3 DROPS CINNAMON OIL

CANCER OIL
BASE OIL
5 DROPS VIOLET OIL
1 DROP LILAC OIL
1 DROP LEMON OIL
3 DROPS AMBERGRIS OIL

GEMINI OIL
BASE OIL
3 DROPS LAVENDER OIL
2 DROPS PEPPERMINT
3 DROPS ALMOND OIL
2 DROPS LILLY

CAPRICORN OIL
BASE OIL
5 DROPS HONEYSUCKLE
2 DROPS PATCHOULY
1 DROP VETIVERT
2 DROPS CYPRESS

PISCES OIL
BASE OIL
5 DROPS ANISE OIL
1 DROP NUTMEG OIL
1 DROP HONEYSUCKLE OIL
3 DROPS JASMINE OIL

SAGITTARIUS OIL
BASE OIL
7 DROPS ROSE OIL
1 DROP CEDARWOOD OIL
1 DROP GINGER
1 DROP SAGE OIL

TAURUS OIL
BASE OIL
3 DROPS LILAC OIL
2 DROPS VANILLA OIL
3 DROPS ROSE OIL
2 DROPS VIOLET OIL

VIRGO OIL
BASE OIL
2 DROPS LILY OIL
3 DROPS LAVENDER OIL
3 DROPS HONEYSUCKLE OIL
2 DROPS BERGAMOT OIL

SCORPIO OIL
BASE OIL
2 DROPS AMBERGRIS OIL
3 DROPS VIOLET OIL
3 DROPS GARDENIA OIL
2 DROPS CLOVE OIL

LEO OIL
BASE OIL
3 DROPS ROSEMARY OIL
5 DROPS MUSK OIL
2 DROPS CINNAMON OIL
1 DROP ACACIA OIL

COME TO ME OIL
BASE OIL
3 DROPS CINNAMON OIL
2 DROPS YLANG YLANG OIL
2 DROPS VANILLA OIL
3 DROPS AMBERGRIS OIL

CONQUERING OIL
BASE OIL
3 DROPS ALLSPICE OIL
3 DROPS VANILLA OIL
3 DROPS CINNAMON OIL
1 DROP DRAGON'S BLOOD OIL

GOLD AND SILVER OIL
BASE OIL
5 DROPS CINNAMON OIL
1 DROP CLOVE OIL
3 DROPS PEPPERMINT OIL
1 DROP ALMOND OIL

GET RID OF EVIL OIL
BASE OIL
3 DROPS DRAGON'S BLOOD OIL
1 DROP MISTLETOE OIL
3 DROPS ANGELICA OIL
3 DROPS PEPPERMINT OIL

SPELL BREAKING OIL
BASE OIL
3 DROPS SANDLEWOOD OIL
1 DROP MYRRH
3 DROPS LILAC OIL
3 DROPS ANISE OIL

STEADY WORK OIL
BASE OIL
3 DROPS HEATHER OIL
2 DROPS VIOLET OIL
1 DROP ROSE OIL
4 DROPS VETIVERT OIL

HEALING OIL
BASE OIL
5 DROPS COCONUT OIL
1 DROP EUCALYPTUS OIL
1 DROP SANDALWOOD OIL
3 DROPS VIOLET OIL

LUCKY DICE OIL
BASE OIL
2 DROPS ANISE OIL
3 DROPS JASMINE OIL
2 DROPS PATCHOULY OIL
3 DROPS CARNATION OIL

SEPARATION OIL
BASE OIL
3 DROPS VETIVERT OIL
3 DROPS SANDLEWOOD OIL
1 DROP CLOVE OIL
4 DROPS BLACK PEPPER OIL

QUICK MARRIAGE OIL
BASE OIL
3 DROPS LAVENDER OIL
3 DROPS VANILLA OIL
3 DROPS AMBERGRIS OIL
1 DROP PEPPERMINT OIL

PROSPERITY OIL
BASE OIL
3 DROPS VIOLET OIL
1 DROP ROSE OIL
4 DROPS CINNAMON OIL
3 DROPS PINE OIL

BETTER BUSINESS OIL
BASE OIL
3 DROPS COCONUT OIL
2 DROPS HYSSOP OIL
3 DROPS VIOLET OIL
2 DROPS HEATHER OIL

DO AS I SAY OIL
BASE OIL
5 DROPS VANILLA OIL
3 DROPS AMBERGRIS OIL
1 DROP ROSEMARY OIL
1 DROP FRANKINCENSE OIL

BANISHING OIL
BASE OIL
3 DROPS MYRRH OIL
2 DROPS FRANKINCENSE OIL
3 DROPS DRAGON'S BLOOD OIL
2 DROPS PEPPERMINT OIL

APHRODISIAC OIL
BASE OIL
5 DROPS AMBERGRIS OIL
7 DROPS HISBISCUS OIL
3 DROPS VANILLA OIL
4 DROPS CINNAMON OIL

DOMINATION OIL
BASE OIL
7 DROPS VANILLA OIL
3 DROPS VIOLET OIL
3 DROPS ALLSPICE OIL
2 DROPS YLANG YLANG OIL

COURT VICTORY OIL
BASE OIL
3 DROPS CAMPHOR OIL
5 DROPS NUTMEG OIL
3 DROPS PEPPERMINT OIL
2 DROPS SAGE OIL

QUEEN CLEOPATRA ATTRACTION OIL
BASE OIL
5 DROPS CINNAMON OIL
2 DROPS VIOLET OIL
3 DROPS AMBERGRIS OIL
1 DROP PEPPERMINT OIL
3 DROPS VANILLA OIL

FAST MONEY OIL
BASE OIL
5 DROPS NUTMEG OIL
3 DROPS HYSSOP OIL
3 DROPS HONEYSUCKLE OIL
1 DROP CINNAMON OIL

CONFUSION OIL
BASE OIL
5 DROPS COCONUT OIL
3 DROPS LAVENDER OIL
2 DROPS VIOLET OIL
3 DROPS BLACK PEPPER OIL
2 DROPS GINSENG OIL

FAST LUCK OIL
BASE OIL
5 DROPS PATCHOULY OIL
2 DROPS PINE OIL
1 DROP VETIVERT OIL
5 DROPS CINNAMON OIL

ATTRACTION OIL
BASE OIL
5 DROPS VANILLA OIL
3 DROPS TUBEROSE OIL
1 DROP PEPPERMINT
1 DROP ROSEMARY

BIG MONEY OIL
BASE OIL
3 DROPS CARNATION OIL
3 DROPS VANILLA OIL
2 DROPS LILAC OIL
2 DROPS SASSAFRAS OIL

LUCKY LOTTO OIL
BASE OIL
3 DROPS ALLSPICE OIL
2 DROPS CEDARZOOOD OIL
1 DROP SAGE OIL
4 DROPS CLOVER OIL

CHIEF CRAZY HORSE VICTORY OIL
BASE OIL
3 DROPS GARDENIA OIL
3 DROPS VIOLET OIL
2 DROPS PEPPERMINT OIL
2 DROPS CIVET OIL

CROSSING OIL
BASE OIL
3 DROPS TANGERINE OIL
4 DROPS VANILLA OIL
3 DROPS RED PEPPER OIL
3 DROPS BLACK PEPPER OIL

UNCROSSING OIL
BASE OIL
3 DROPS COCONUT OIL
3 DROPS SAGE OIL
3 DROPS LILAC OIL
2 DROP MYRRH OIL
1 DROP FRANKINCENSE OIL

JUST JUDGE OIL
BASE OIL
3 DROPS DRAGON'S BLOOD OIL
2 DROPS HYACINTH OIL
3 DROPS RUE OIL
2 DROPS PENNYROYAL OIL
2 DROPS MANDRAKE OIL

LOVE DROPS
BASE OIL
5 DROPS CINNAMON OIL
2 DROPS PATCHOULY OIL
3 DROPS VANILLA OIL
1 DROP PEPPERMINT OIL
1 DROP CIVET OIL

HOT FOOT OIL
BASE OIL
7 DROPS BLACK PEPPER OIL
7 DROPS RED PEPPER OIL
3 DROPS PEPPERMINT OIL
2 DROPS VANILLA OIL

MONEY DRAWING OIL
BASE OIL
7 DROPS LAVENDER OIL
3 DROPS PATCHOULY OIL
4 DROPS HONEYSUCKLE OIL
2 DROPS MAGNOLIA OIL

REVERSIBLE OIL
BASE OIL
7 DROPS BASIL OIL
2 DROPS PINE OIL
3 DROPS GINGER OIL
3 DROPS DRAGON'S BLOOD OIL

ABRE CAMINO
ROAD OPENER OIL
BASE OIL
7 DROPS ANISE OIL
3 DROPS SASSAFRAS OIL
2 DROPS NUTMEG OIL
3 DROPS HYSSOP OIL

HOLD MY MAN OIL
BASE OIL
2 DROPS ORIS OIL
3 DROPS PLUMERIA OIL
3 DROPS TUBEROSE OIL
1 DROP YANG YLANG OIL

HOLD MY WOMAN OIL
BASE OIL
4 DROPS ROSE OIL
3 DROPS VIOLET OIL
1 DROP SPEARMINT OIL
3 DROPS APPLE OIL

GUARDIAN ANGEL OIL
BASE OIL
7 DROPS COCONUT OIL
3 DROPS NUTMEG OIL
2 DROPS CINNAMON OIL
1 DROP PEPPERMINT OIL

LAW STAY AWAY OIL
BASE OIL
3 DROPS SAGE OIL
3 DROPS HYSSOP OIL
1 DROP ANISE OIL
2 DROPS HONEYSUCKLE OIL

HUMMINGBIRD
(CHUPAROSSA) OIL
BASE OIL
5 DROPS HONEYSUCKLE OIL
2 DROPS CINNAMON OIL
3 DROPS ROSE OIL
2 DROPS PLUMERIA OIL
1 DROP LILAC OIL

JINX OIL
BASE OIL
7 DROPS HEMLOCK OIL
3 DROPS CORIANDER OIL
2 DROPS ALLSPICE OIL
2 DROPS BLACK PEPPER OIL
1 DROP GINGER OIL

HIGH JOHN THE CONQUEROR OIL
BASE OIL
3 DROPS LAVENDER OIL
2 DROPS DRAGON'S BLOOD OIL
3 DROPS YLANG YLANG OIL
2 DROPS PATCHOULY OIL

7 DAY QUICK UNCROSSING OIL
BASE OIL
7 DROPS COCONUT OIL
2 DROPS LAVENDER OIL
2 DROPS DRAGON'S BLOOD OIL
2 DROPS CLOVE OIL

STEADY WORK OIL
BASE OIL
3 DROPS LERNONGRASS OIL
2 DROPS SAGE OIL
1 DROP HYSSOP OIL
2 DROPS ROSE OIL

LUCKY GAMBLER OIL
BASE OIL
5 DROPS CINNAMON OIL
3 DROPS JASMINE OIL
2 DROPS ROSE OIL
1 DROP HONEYSUCKLE OIL

BALSAMO TRANQUILO OIL
BASE OIL
4 DROPS BALSAM OIL
3 DROPS ROSE OIL
2 DROPS VANILLA OIL
3 DROPS LAVENDER OIL

BALSAMO INTRANQUILO OIL
BASE OIL
4 DROPS BALSAM OIL
3 DROPS BLACK PEPPER OIL
2 DROPS GINGER OIL
1 DROP BAY OIL

SEVEN INDIAN SPIRITS OIL
BASE OIL
2 DROPS TANGERINE OIL
3 DROPS GRAPE OIL
4 DROPS PINE OIL
2 DROPS ORCHID OIL
1 DROP PEPPERMINT OIL

SAN MARTIN CABALLERO BUSINESS OIL
BASE OIL
5 DROPS ALMOND OIL
1 DROP HYSSOP OIL
1 DROP CARNATION OIL
2 DROPS HEATHER OIL

LA SANTISIMA MUERTE DOMINATION OIL
BASE OIL
4 DROPS HIBISCUS OIL
2 DROPS LIME OIL
1 DROP HEATHER OIL
3 DROPS CINNAMON OIL
4 DROPS HIGH JOHN THE
  CONQUEROR ROOT OIL

SAN ALEJO PROTECTION OIL
BASE OIL
3 DROPSDRAGON'S BLOOD OIL
3 DROPS SAGE OIL
2 DROPS JUNIPER OIL
2 DROPS ROSEMARY OIL
1 DROP SANDLEWOOD OIL

SAN SIMON LOVE OIL
BASE OIL
2 DROPS PALMAROSA OIL
3 DROPS VIOLET OIL
3 DROPS CINNAMON OIL
3 DROPS AMBERGRIS OIL

SAN SIMON REVERSE OIL
BASE OIL
3 DROPS CARNATION OIL
3 DROPS COCONUT OIL
2 DROPS DRAGON'S BLOOD OIL
2 DROPS MYRRH OIL

HAITAN VOODOO DESTRUCTION OIL
BASE OIL
7 DROPS BLACK PEPPER OIL
3 DROPS RED CHILE PEPPER OIL
3 DROPS MISTLETOE OIL
4 DROPS ALLSPICE OIL
1 DROP COFFEE OIL

CANDOMBLE SPIRIT OIL
BASE OIL
4 DROPS FRANKINCENSE OIL
7 DROPS CINNAMON OIL
3 DROPS ORANGE OIL
1 DROP LOTUS OIL

KEEP MOUTH SHUT OIL
BASE OIL
7 DROPS COCONUT OIL
7 DROPS BLACK PEPPER OIL
3 DROPS ANISE OIL
1 DROP SASSAFRAS OIL

GET OUT OF JAIL OIL
BASE OIL
7 DROPS DRAGON'S BLOOD OIL
21 DROPS COCONUT OIL
7 DROPS NUTMEG OIL

LUST OIL
BASE OIL
5 DROPS CINNAMON OIL
2 DROPS PACHOULY OIL
2 DROPS AMBERGRIS OIL
4 DROPS VANILLA OIL
1 DROP HIBISCUS OIL

HIGH ALTAR PURIFICATION OIL
BASE OIL
3 DROPS SAGE OIL
3 DROPS CAMPHOR OIL
1 DROP ROSE OIL
2 DROPS SANDALWOOD OIL

SEVEN HOLY KINGS VICTORY OIL
BASE OIL
3 DROPS PINE OIL
2 DROPS VIOLET OIL
3 DROPS WINTERGREEN OIL
1 DROP HYSSOP OIL
2 DROPS VANILLA OIL

6

SANTERIA OIL LAMPS

Oil lamps have been used for centuries in temples around the world. Oil lamps are an effective way to petition the Orishas for blessings and special requests. Oil lamps can contain a multitude of ingredients that are neccessary to bring forth magic. The following oil lamp formulas have been taken from original magic manuscripts used by my family for many years with great success. Some of the formulas have been altered in order to accomodate the modern day practioner of Santeria.

OCHUN'S OIL LAMP
This oil lamp is used for special requests

INGREDIENTS

1. *Vanilla Flan (Spanish Custard)*
2. *1 tablespoon Cinnamon Powder*
3. *1 tablespoon Honey*
4. *1 tablespoon Corn Meal*
5. *1/4 cup River Water*
6. *1 cup Almond Oil*
7. *1 tbsp. Yellow Precipitate Powder*
8. *One Floating Nite Light*

PREPARATION

1. *Write your name five times on a piece of brown paper and place it at the bottom of a white bowl.*
2. *Place the flan on top of the brown paper.*

3. *Pour the honey over the flan.*
4. *Sprinkle the cinnamon and the corn meal over the honey.*
5. *Pour the River Water around the flan.*
6. *Add the Almond Oil to the bowl.*
7. *Mix the Yellow Precipitate into the Almond Oil.*
8. *Float the Nite Light on the oil and light for five consecutive days. On the 6th day place the lamp on river bank with five cents.*

YEMAYA'S OIL LAMP #1

This oil lamp is used for special requests

INGREDIENTS

1. One Cantaloupe
2. 1 tablespoon Orange Water
3. 1 tablespoon Sea Water
4. 1 tablespoon River Water
5. 1 tablespoon Florida Water
6. 1 tablespoon Anil Powder
7. 1 cup Almond Oil
8. One floating Nite Light

PREPARATION

1. *Cut a medium size hole into a Cantaloupe Melon.*
2. *Empty the seeds from the Cantaloupe.*
3. *Write your name seven times on a brown piece of paper and place at the bottom of the Cantaloupe.*
4. *Pour the Orange Water, Sea Water, River Water and the Florida Water into the Cantaloupe.*
5. *Add the Almond Oil to the Cantaloupe.*
6. *Mix the Anil powder with the oil.*
7. *Float the Nite Light in the center of the Cantaloupe and light for 7 consecutive days. On the 8th day, take the lamp to the ocean, place it on the beach with 7 pennies.*

YEMAYA'S OIL LAMP #2
This oil lamp is used for special requests.

INGREDIENTS

1. One Medium Size Bowl
2. 1 tablespoon Pork Lard
3. 1 tablespoon Palm Oil
4. 1 tablespoon Brown Sugar
5. 1 tablespoon Cocoa Butter
6. 1 tablespoon Anil Powder
7. 1 tablespoon Sea Salt
8. 1 tablespoon Corn Meal
9. 2 cups Coconut Oil
10. One Floating Night Light

PREPARATION

1. Write your name seven times on a brown piece of paper and place at the bottom of the bowl.
2. Pour the Pork Lard, Palm Oil, Brown Sugar, Cocoa Butter, Sea Salt
3. and the Corn Meal over the paper.
4. Pour the Coconut Oil into the bowl.
5. Mix the Anil powder with the Coconut Oil.
6. Float the Nite Light on the top of the oil.
7. Light the Nite Light for seven consecutive days. On the 8th day, wrap the lamp with a blue cloth and leave it on the beach by the ocean along with 7 pennies.

ELEGGUA'S OIL LAMP #1
This oil lamp is used for special requests.

INGREDIENTS

1. Coconut
2. 1 tblsp. Pwdrd. Palo Abre Camino
3. 1 tblsp. Pwdrd. Palo Guayaba
4. 1 tablespoon Honey
4. 1 cup Coconut Oil
5. 1 tblsp. White Precip. Pwdr.
6. 1 floating Nite Light

PREPARATION

1. Cut a large hole in a coconut.
2. Write your name three times on a piece of brown paper and place it at the bottom of the coconut.
3. Take a mouthful of rum and spray it directly into the coconut.
4. Light a cigar and blow the smoke directly into the coconut.

5. Add the honey and both of the powdered palos into the coconut.
6. Add the oil and White Precipitate powder to the coconut.
7. Place the floating Night Light into the coconut and light for three consecutive days.
8. On the 4th day take the coconut to a crossroad and leave with 21 pennies.

ELEGGUA'S OIL LAMP #2
This oil lamp is used to attract love.

INGREDIENTS

1. One Medium Size White Bowl
2. 1 tblsp. Pwdrd. Palo Ven A Mi
3. 1 tblsp. Pwdrd. Palo Amansa Guapo
4. 1 tblsp. Pwdrd. Palo Abre Camino

5. 1 tblsp. Rum
6. 1 tblsp. each of 3 types of Dry Wine
7. 2 cups Coconut Oil
8. One floating Nite Light

PREPARATION

1. Write the name of the desired individual three times on a piece of brown paper. Write your name three times directly accross the other name. The names will intersect forming a cross. Place the paper at the bottom of the bowl.
2. Pour the Rum and the three types of Dry Wine over the paper.
3. Sprinkle all of powdered Palos over the paper.
4. Add the Coconut Oil to the bowl.
5. Float the Nite Light on the oil and light for three consecutive days.
6. On the 4th day, wrap the lamp in a white cloth with 3 pennies and place it at a street intersection near the home of the desired individual.

OCHUN'S ATTRACTION OIL LAMP

This Oil Lamp is used to bring prosperity to an individual.

INGREDIENTS

1. One medium Pumpkin
2. 1 tblsp. ground Cinnamon
3. 1 tblsp. of Pwdrd. Palo Amansa Guapo
4. 1 tblsp. of Powdered PaloVen A Mi
5. Two cups of Almond Oil
6. Five different Love Oils
7. One Nickel
8. Five Gold Fishing Hooks
9. 2 tblsp. Honey
10. 2 tblsp. Brown Sugar
11. 1 tblsp. Red Precip. Pwdr.
12. One floating Nite Light

PREPARATION

1. Cut the top off the pumpkin and empty the insides.
2. Write the name of the desired individual five times on a brown piece of paper. Write your name across the other individuals name five times.
3. The names should intersect forming a cross.
4. Insert the fishing hooks through the paper.
5. Place the paper into the bottom of the pumpkin. The names should be facing up.
6. Place the nickels in the center of the paper, along with five pumpkin seeds.
7. Sprinkle the cinnamon on the paper.
8. Pour the honey in the pumpkin.
9. Add all of the powdered palos to the pumpkin.
10. Add the brown sugar to the pumpkin.
11. Add the almond oil to the pumpkin.
12. Add all of the love oils to the pumpkin.
13. Add the red precipitate powder to the oil and mix well.
14. Place the floating Nite Lite on top of the oil mixture.
15. Light the Nite Light for five consecutive days.
16. On the 6th day, place the pumpkin by a running stream or river.

OCHUN'S PROSPERITY OIL LAMP

This oil lamp is used to bring prosperity to an individual.

INGREDIENTS

1. One medium size pumpkin
2. 1 tblsp. Pwdrd. Palo Abre Camino
3. 1 tblsp. Cinnamon Powder
4. 1 tblsp. Pwdrd. Palo Dulce
5. 1 tblsp. Pwdrd. Palo Guayaba
6. 1 tablespoon Deerhorn Powder
7. 1 tblsp. Red Precip. Powder
8. 5 tblsp. Honey
9. Five Nickels
10. Five Gold Fishing Hooks
11. Five different Money Oils
12. 2 Cups Almond Oil

PREPARATION

1. Cut the top off the pumpkin and empty the insides.
2. Write your name five times on a brown piece of paper.
3. Insert the fishing hooks through the paper.
4. Place the paper into the bottom of the pumpkin. The name should be face up.
5. Place the pickles on the paper.
6. Place 25 pumpkin seeds on the paper.
7. Add the powdered Palo Abre Camino in the pumpkin.
8. Place the Cinnamon Powder in the pumpkin.
9. Place the powdered Palo Dulce in the pumpkin.
10. Place the powdered Palo Guayaba in the pumpkin.
11. Place the Deerhorn powder in the pumpkin.
12. Pour the honey over all of the ingredients.
13. Add the Almond Oil into the pumpkin.
14. Mix the Red Precipitate powder into the oil mixture.
15. Add the five money oils to the oil mixture.
16. Place the floating Nite Light on top of the oil.
17. Light the Nite Light for five consecutive days.
18. On the 6th day, place the pumpkin into a running stream or river.

YEMAYA'S FERTILITY OIL LAMP

This oil lamp is used to bring fertility and protection to women.
This oil lamp is also used for special requests.

INGREDIENTS

1. One Watermelon
2. 1 tblsp. Pwdrd. Palo Dulce
3. 1 cup mixed Rice & Beans (Dried)
4. 1tblsp. shredded Coconut
5. 2 tblsp. fresh Basil Leaves
6. 1 tblsp. Anil Powder
7. 1 tblsp. River Water

8. 1 tblsp. Sea Water
9. 2 cups Molassas
10. 3 cups Olive Oil
11. 7 Pennies
12. 1 tblsp. White Precip. Pwdr.
13. 1 floating Nite Light

PREPARATION

1. Cut watermelon in two parts. Scope the majority of the insides out.
2. Write your name seven times on a brown piece of paper. Place the paper at the bottom of the watermelon.
3. Place the seven pennies on the paper.
4. Place seven watermelon seeds on the paper.
5. Place the powdered Palo Dulce, rice and beans, shredded coconut and the fresh basil leaves in the watermelon.
6. Pour the River Water and the Sea Water into the watermelon.
7. Pour the Molassas into the watermelon.
8. Pour the Olive Oil into the watermelon.
9. Mix the Anil and White Precipitate powder into the olive oil.
10. Float the Nite Light on top of the oil.
11. Light the Nite Light and allow it to burn for seven consecutive days.
12. On the 8th day leave the Oil Lamp on the beach near the ocean.

CHANGO'S VICTORY OIL LAMP

This oil lamp is used to bring an individual the power to
overcome enemies and difficult obstacles.

INGREDIENTS

1. One large ceremic bowl
2. Palmagranet Juice
3. Clove Powder
4. Sliced Plantano
5. Sliced Red Apples

6. Powdered Palo Vence Batalla
7. Cinnamon Powder
8. Honey
9. Red Wine
10. 6 Pennies

11. 1 tablespoon Red Precipitate Powder
12. 2 cups Olive Oil
13. 1 floating Nite Light

PREPARATION

1. *Write your name six times on a piece of brown paper and place it at the bottom of the bowl and place the six pennies on the paper.*
2. *Pour the Palmagranant Juice over the paper.*
3. *Place six pieces of sliced Plantano and six pieces of sliced Red Apple in the bowl.*
4. *Sprinkle the powdered Palo Vence Batalla, Clove powder and the Cinnamon powder on the fruit.*
5. *Pour the honey over the ingredients in the bowl.*
6. *Pour the red wine in the bowl.*
7. *Pour the Olive Oil in the bowl.*
8. *Mix the Red Precipitate Powder with the oil.*
9. *Float the Nite Light on the oil and light for six consecutive days.*
10. *On the 7th day wrap the lamp with a red cloth and leave in a wooded area.*

7 AFRICAN POWERS OIL LAMP
This oil lamp is used for special requests.

INGREDIENTS

1. *One Large Bowl*
2. *1 cup Almond Oil*
3. *1 tblsp. Palm Oil*
4. *1 cup Coconut Oil*
5. *1 tblsp.Coco Butter*
6. *1 tblsp. Red Wine*
7. *1 tblsp. Rum*
8. *1 tblsp. Anisette Liquor*
9. *1 tblsp. Cognac*
10. *1 tblsp. Gin*
11. *1 tblsp. Azucena Water*
12. *1 tblsp. Seseme Seeds*
13. *Seven Carmel Candies*
14. *1/4 teaspoon Black Pepper*
15. *1 tblsp.Balsamo Tranquilo Oil*
16. *7 Lode Stones w/ Magnetic Sand*
17. *1 tblsp. Red Precipitate Powder*
18. *Seven Floating Night Lights*

PREPARATION

1. Write your name seven times on a brown piece of paper. Place the paper at the bottom of the bowl.
2. Place the seven Lode Stones and Magnetic Sand directly on the paper.
3. Place the seven Caramel candies around the Lode Stones and sand.
4. In a separate bowl mix all of the other listed ingredients together and then pour over the Lode Stones.
5. Float the seven Nite Lights on the oil mixture and light all of them for seven consecutive days.
6. On the 8th day, place the lamp on the beach by the ocean with seven pennies.

OCHOSI'S OIL LAMP

This oil lamp is used to win a court battle or to free someone from jail.

INGREDIENTS

1. One Medium Size Bowl
2. 1 cup Anisette Liquor
3. 2 Sticks of Rock Candy
4. 1 tablespoon Deerhorn Powder
5. Powdered Palo Abre Camino
6. 2 cups Coconut Oil
7. 1 tblsp. Red Precip. Powder
8. Four Metal Crossbows of Ochosi
9. One Floating Night Light

PREPARATION

1. Write the individuals name three times on a piece of brown paper and place the paper at the bottom of the bowl.
2. Place the four metal Crossbows around the paper.
3. Sprinkle the powdered Palo Abre Camino, powdered Palo Justicia and the Deerhorn powder over the paper.
5. Place the Rock Candy in the bowl.
6. Pour the Anisette Liquor on the ingredients.
7. Pour the Coconut Oil into the bowl.
8. Mix the Red Precipitate Powder into the oil.
9. Float the Nite Light on the oil and light for seven consecutive days before the court date or hearing.
10. On the 8th day, discard the lamp near the court building.

OGGUN'S OIL LAMP

This lamp is used for special requests.

INGREDIENTS

1. One Cast Iron Cauldron
2. 1 cup Honey
3. 2 tablespoons Palm Oil
4. Rum
5. Cigar
6. 3 tablespoons Magnetic Sand
7. 1 tablespoon Smoked Fish
8. 1 tablespoon Smoked Possum
9. 3 pieces of Alum
10. 3 cups Olive Oil
11. One Floating Nite Light

PREPARATION

1. Spray a mouthful of rum directly in the cauldron three times.
2. Blow cigar smoke direcly into the cauldron three times.
3. Place the Magnetic Sand at the bottom of the cauldron.
4. Add the Smoked Fish and Smoked Possum to the cauldron.
5. Place the Alum into the center of the cauldron.
6. Pour the Palm Oil and Honey over all of the ingredients.
7. Pour the oil in the cauldron.
8. Float the Nite Light on the oil and light for 27 consecutive days.
9. On the 28th day, pour out the ingredients at the railroad tracks.

MONEY ATTRACTION LAMP

This oil lamp is used to attract money to a home or business.

INGREDIENTS

1. One Medium Bowl
2. 1 tablespoon Palm Oil
3. 2 tablespoon Honey
4. 1 tablespoon Cognac
5. 1 tablespoon Sugar
6. Five Pieces of Fool's Gold
7. 2 cups Almond Oil
8. One Floating Nite Light

PREPARATION

1. Place the Fool's Gold in the bottom of the bowl.
2. Pour the Honey over the stones.
3. Add the Palm Oil, Cognac and the sugar to the bowl.
4. Pour the oil into the bowl.
5. Float the Nite Light on the oil and light for five days.
6. On the 6th day, wrap the lamp in a gold cloth and leave it on a river bank.

GAMBLER'S LUCK LAMP

This oil lamp is used to attract money and luck in gambling.

INGREDIENTS

1. One medium size bowl
2. 5 pieces of High John the Conqueror Root
3. 1 tblsp. Cinnamon Powder
4. 1 tblsp. Abre Camino Herb
5. 1 tblsp. Deerhorn Powder
6. 1 tablespoon Honey
7. 1/4 ounce Money Drawing Oil
8. 1/4 ounce Lucky Gambling Oil
9. 3 cups Almond Oil
10. One Floating Nite Light

PREPARATION

1. Place the High John the Conqueror Root in the bowl.
2. Sprinkle the Cinnamon Powder, Deerhorn Powder and the Abre Camino
3. Herb into the bowl.
   Pour the Honey over the ingredients in the bowl.
4. Mix the Money Drawing Oil and the Lucky Gambler Oil with the Almond Oil and pour over the ingredients in the bowl.
5. Float the Nite Light on the oil and light for seven consecutive days.
6. On the 8th day, pour the ingredients of the lamp on the ground at a crossroads.

PEACE & TRANQUILITY LAMP

This oil lamp is used to pacify an enemy.

INGREDIENTS

1. One Medium Size Bowl
2. 1 tblsp. Honey
3. 1 tblsp. Red Precíp. Powder
4. 1 tblsp. Yellow Precip. Powder
5. 1 tblsp. White Precip. Powder
6. 1 tblsp. Pwdrd. Palo Amansa Guapo
7. 1 tblsp. Pwdrd. Palo Para Mi
8. 1 ounce Balsamo Tranquilo Oil
9. 2 cups Almond Oil
10. One Floating Nite Light

PREPARATION

1. Write the individuals name on a piece of brown paper six times.
2. Place the paper at the bottom of the bowl.
3. Pour the Honey over the paper.
4. Sprinkle the Palo Amansa Guapo and Palo Para Mi over the Honey.

5. *Mix the Balsamo Tranquilo Oil, Red Precipitate Powder, Yellow Precipitate Powder and the White Precipitate Powder with the Almond Oil.*
6. *Pour the oil mixture into the bowl.*
7. *Float the Nite Light on the oil and light for 14 consecutive days.*
8. *On the 15th day, leave the remaining contents near your enemies home or business.*

PALO MAYOMBE DESTRUCTION LAMP

This oil lamp is used to destroy an enemy.

INGREDIENTS

1. *One Large Cast Iron Cauldron*
2. *1 cup Vinegar*
3. *1 tblsp. Black Salt*
4. *9 Pins*
5. *1 tblsp. Red Wine*
6. *Rum*
7. *Cigar*
8. *1 tblsp. Black Pepper*
9. *1 tblsp. Red Chile Pepper Pwdr.*
10. *1 cup Dirt from the grave of a murdered person*
11. *1 tblsp. Scorpion Powder*
12. *1 tblsp. Powder of the Dead*
13. *1/2 cup Snake Oil*
14. *1 tblsp. Pwdrd. Palo Muerto*
15. *1 tblsp. Powdered Palo Cambia Rumba*
16. *3 cups Cooking Oil*
17. *1 tblsp. Black Precip. Powder*
18. *1 tblsp. Red Precip. Powder*
19. *Nine Floating Nite Lights*

PREPARATION

1. *Write the individuals name nine times on a piece of brown paper. Write the individuals name nine more times the opposite way to form a cross.*
2. *Pierce the pins through the paper and place it at the bottom of the cauldron.*
3. *Take a mouthful of rum and spray it into the cauldron three times.*
4. *Light a cigar and blow the smoke directly on the paper.*
5. *Pour the Snake Oil over the paper.*
6. *Sprinkle the Powder of the Dead and the Scorpion Powder over the paper.*
7. *Sprinkle the Black Pepper,Red Chile Powder,powdered Palo Muerto and the powdered Palo Cambia Rumba over the other ingredients.*
8. *Pour the Vinegar and the Red Wine around the ingredients.*
9. *Sprinkle the Cemetery Dirt over all of the other ingredients to form a mound.*

10. Mix the Black Precipitate Powder and the Red Precipitate Powder with the cooking oil and then pour into the cauldron.
11. Float the nine Nite Lights on the oil and then light for nine consecutive days and nights.
12. On the 10th day, take the remaining liquid mixture and bury over a grave with nine pennies.

PALO MAYOMBE CONFLICT LAMP

This oil lamp is used to bring conflict between two individuals.

INGREDIENTS

1. 1 medium size Cast Iron Cauldron
2. 1 tblsp. Pwdrd. Palo Cambia Rumba
3. 1 tblsp. Pwdrd. Palo Vence Batalla
4. 1 tblsp. Pwdrd. Palo Muerto
5. 1 ounce Black Dog Hair
6. 1 ounce Black Cat Hair
7. 1 tspn. Pwdrd. Rooster's fighting Spur
8. 1 tblsp. Pwdrd. Bat
9. Nine Pins
10. 1 tblsp. Red Precip. Powder
11. 3 cups Cooking Oil
12. Nine Floating Nite Lights

PREPARATION

1. Write the individuals name nine times on a brown piece of paper. Write the other individuals name nine times forming a cross.
2. Pierce the pins through the paper and place it at the bottom of the caudron.
3. Sprinkle the Black Dog's Hair and the Black Cat's Hair over the paper.
4. Sprinkle all of the powdered palos on the paper.
5. Sprinkle the powdered Bat and the powdered Rooster's Fighting Spur over the other ingredients.
6. Mix the Red Precipitate Powder with the cooking oil and pour into the cauldron.
7. Float the nine Nite Lights on the oil and light for nine days.
8. On the 10th day, bury the remaining liquid over a grave with 9 pennies.

PALO MAYOMBE REVERSE LAMP

*This oil lamp is used to reverse witchcraft
or to get rid of an evil spirit.*

INGREDIENTS

1. One Medium Cast Iron Cauldron
2. 1 tablespoon fresh Garlic
3. 1 tblsp. Pwdrd. Palo Espanta Muerto
4. 1 tblsp. Pwdrd. Palo Caballero
5. 1 tblsp. Pwdrd. Palo Canpeche
6. 1 cup fresh Rue
7. 1 cup fresh Rosemary
8. 1 ounce Dragon's Blood Oil
9. 1 tblsp. Deerhorn Powder
10. 3 cups Olive Oil
11. 1 tblsp. White Precip. Powder
12. Nine Floating Nite Lights

PREPARATION

1. Place the fresh Rue and Rosemary in the cauldron.
2. Sprinkle all of the powdered pales in the cauldron.
3. Sprinkle the Garlic powder and Deerhorn powder into the cauldron.
4. Mix the Dragon's Blood Oil and the White Precipitate Powder with the Olive Oil and then pour over the other ingredients in the cauldron.
5. Float the nine Nite Lights on the oil and then light for 9 consecutive days.
6. On the 10th day, leave the remaining liquid on the beach by the ocean with seven pennies.

7

7 DAY CANDLES

The use of 7 Day Glass Candles by spiritualists in the Santeria religion is quite common. Botanicas carry a vast array of these candles. Glass candles come in a variety of colors and designs. Each candle has a specific purpose. The following is a list of 7 Day Glass Candles most commonly used with their names, meanings and specific magical usages

PLAIN SOLID COLORED CANDLES

GREEN - Green candles are used for money and prosperity spells. Green candles are also attributed to the Seven African Powers.

RED - Red candles are used in love and domination spells. Red candles are attributed to the Orisha Chango.

YELLOW - Yellow candles are used in love and health spells. Yellow candles are associated with the Orishas Ochun and Babalu-Aye.

WHITE - White candles are used to bring peace and communition with our guardian angels. White candle are associated with the Orisha Obatala.

BLUE - Blue candles are used to bring an individual peace and tranquility. Blue candles are associated with the Orisha Yemaya.

PURPLE - Purple candles are used for power and strength. Purple candles are associated with the Orishas Ochosi and San Lazaro.

GOLD - Gold candles are associated with power and prosperity. Gold candles are associated with Olodumare (God).

SILVER - Silver candles are used to represent protection and stability. Silver candles are associated with the Orisha Olocun.

BROWN - Brown candles are associated with fertility and the harvest. Brown candles are associated with the Orishas Oya and Oko.

BLACK - Black candles are used for destruction and communication with the spirits of the night.

ORANGE - Orange candles are used for protection and for power.

PINK - Pink candles are used in love spells and to bring peace to an unhappy home or location.

TWO TONED
COLORED CANDLES

BLACK/RED - This candle is used to reverse witchcraft or negativity. This candle is associated with the Orisha Eleggua.

GREEN/YELLOW - This candle is used for prosperity and for clear spiritual divination. This candle is associated with the Orisha Orunla.

WHITE/BLUE - This candle is used to bring peace to a home. It is also used in fertility spells.

BLACK/GREEN - This candle is used for protection and in spells of Divine Justice. This candle is associated with the Orisha Oggun and the Spirit Zarabanda.

YELLOW/RED - This candle is used in love spells. The candle represents the union of the Orishas Ochun and Chango.

SPECIALTY & ILLUSTRATED CANDLES

SEVEN AFRICAN POWERS - This candle is used for blessings, protection and special requests.

ELEGGUA - This candle is used to bring success and opportunities.

YEMAYA - This candle is used for blessings and peace of mind.

CONGO MACHO - This candle is used for protection and blessings.

SANTA BARBARA - This candle is used to dominate and conquer your enemies.

SANTO NINO ATOCHA - This candle is used for special requests and to open the doors to success.

SAN MIGUEL ARCHANGEL - This candle is used to reverse the evil eye and to destroy your enemies.

SAN RAMON - This candle is used to stop your enemies from gossiping.

SAN SIMON - This candle is used for divine justice and special requests.

LA SANTISIMA MUERTE - This candle is used for Divine Justice and special requests.

SAN MARTIN DE PORRES - This candle is used for spiribual communication and psychic powers.

SAN ALEJO - This candle is used to get rid of your enemies.

SAN MARTIN CABALLERO - This candle is used for success in a business.

SAN JUDAS TADEO - This candle is used to bring an individaul money and luck.

SANTA LUCIA - This candle is used for healing especially for ailments of the eyes.

SANTA CLARA - This candle is used for special requests.

SANTA MARTHA - This candle is used to bring back a lover.

SAN LAZARO - This candle is used to heal extremely sick individuals.

SAN EDUVIGIS - This candle is used for victory in difficult court cases.

SACRED HEART OF JESUS - This candle is used for special requests and difficult problems.

SACRED HEART OF MARY - This candle is used to bring an individual blessings from heaven.

SANTA HELENA - This candle is used to expose and to bring your enemies to justice.

SAINT FRANCIS OF ASSISI - This candle is used to bring peace to an unhappy home.

SAN ANTONIO - This candle is used to open the doors of success and blessings.

SANTA TERESA - This candle is used to bring an individual love.

VIRGIN OF REGLA - This candle is used to bring peace of mind and for special favors.

VIRGIN OF GUADALUPE - This candle is used to defeat your enemies and reverse the evil eye.

VIRGIN OF CARIDAD - This candle is used to bring prosperity and wealth.

VIRGIN OF SAN JUAN - This candle is used for healing and reversing witchcraft.

THE JUST JUDGE - This candle is used to have victory in a court case.

SAN SEBASTIAN - This candle is used to bring luck and prosperity to a business.

SAN DESHACEDOR - This candle is used to reverse and break spells directed toward you.

OUR LADY OF MERCY - This candle is used to bring blessings from heaven.

INFANT OF PRAGUE - This candle is used to prevent sickness especially for small children.

HUMMINGBIRD - This candle is used to reunite lovers.

COME TO ME - This candle is used to bring an individual closer to you for love.

FAST LUCK - This candle is used to bring fast love, money, wealth and success.

SEVEN ANGELS - This candle is used for protection of your home and family.

GUARDIAN ANGELS - This candle is used to bring your guardian angel closer to you.

HIGH JOHN THE CONQUEROR - This candle is used for protection, luck and to dominate your enemies.

BLACK CAT - This candle can be used for both good or evil purposes.

BLOCK BUSTER - This candle is used to destroy unwanted enemies.

HORSESHOE - This candle is used to bring luck and money to gamblers.

MONEY HOUSE BLESSING - This candle is used to bring luck to a home.

MONEY DRAWING - This candle is used to attract money and success.

DOOM CANDLE - This candle is used in spells of harm and destruction.

JINX REMOVING - This candle is used to remove an evil spirit or bad luck.

UNCROSSING - This candle is used to remove and reverse a spell directed to you.

ADAM AND EVE - This candle is used to bind two individuals.

PROTECTION - This candle is used to remove negativity from your home or business.

STEADY WORK - This candle is used to keep an individual from getting laid off.

ALLAN KARDEC - This candle is used for clear spiritual communication.

AJO MACHO - This candle is used for protection from evil spirits or the evil eye.

RUN DEVIL RUN - This candle is used to chase away your enemies.

LUCKY BINGO - This candle is used to bring an individual luck in gambling.

HOLY SPIRIT - This candle is used to bring blessings from heaven.

COURT CASE - This candle is used to win in court.

JOB - This candle is used to help an individual find a job.

TAPA BOCA - This candle is used to keep your enemies from gossiping about you.

BUDDHA - This candle is used to bring wealth and success.

RETIRO - This candle is used to get rid of an unwanted person.

8

INTERPRETATION OF CANDLES

When using 7 Day Religious Candles in magical spells it is important to monitor or interpret each candle as it is burning. There are various ways to interpret a candle spell and its effectiveness. The following are the most common and effective ways to interpret 7 Day Glass Religious Candles. If you follow the below suggestions, you will see fast results in your magical endeavors.

What if the candle explodes?

There are two different ways that a candle can be interpreted if it explodes. The first, if the candle is a reverse or protection candle, this means that the candle prevented something from attacking you. It also means that there is alot of negative energy directed towards you. The second, if the candle is being used to dominate or cause conflict to another individual, it means that the individual has a spiritual protection on themselves. In this particular case, you must immediately light another of the same candle in order to effectively break the persons protection and thus allowing the spell to work effectively.

What if the candle does not burn?

There are two ways to interpret a candle that does not want to burn. The first, if the candle is a prosperity or protection candle, this means that another type of spiritual cleansing must be performed prior to beginning your spell. This must be done in order to remove the negativity from the environment before a candle can be effectively used. This can be done by burning sage or real dragon's blood incense. The second, if the candle is being used to inflict harm or to dominate another individual, another method or type of spell must be used .

What if the candle has a high flame?

If a candle flame burns high and hard, this means that the spell is going to be effective and work fast. If the candle is a protection candle or money drawing candle, it means that your environment is spiritually clean from negative energy. If the candle is being used in a spell of harm or to dominate another individual, this means that the person does not have a spiritual protection and it will not be long before you start to see results.

What if the candle has a low flame?

If the candle is being used as a prosperity candle or luck candle and the candle flame burns low, you should cleanse your environment because there is a little negativity. A floor wash is also reccomended. If the candle being burned to dominate or inflict harm on another individual this means that the individual has a strong spirit and it will take a long time before you start to see results. In this case, you should also start another different type of spell in combination with the prepared candle to see faster results.

What if the candle burns the glass totally black?

If a candle finishes and the entire glass has burned black, this means that there is witchcraft or negativity directed toward you. You must immediately cleanse your environment and light a reverse candle to take it out. If the candle is being used to dominate or inflict harm on another individual, this means that the inidviduals spirit is fighting you and has quite possibly warned the individual of a spiritual attack. Unless the attack is warranted for example in matters of Divine Justice I would recommend stopping because it could reverse on you with extremely disasterous results.

What if the candle burns the top half of the glass black?

If a candle only burns the top part of the glass black this means that the candle spell was met by negativity before it started to work. This can also mean that the negativity around the candle was re-moved and reversed.

What if the candle burns the bottom half of the glass black?

There are two meanings which can be applied to this. The first, if the candle is a prosperity, protection or luck candle, negativity was sent your way and the candle detected it. The second, if the candle was being used to harm or dominate another individual, the spirit of the individual was alarmed and has reversed the spell. It would almost be impossible to start another work of any type once the individual knows and has protection.

What if the candle only burns on one side?

This means that the spell will only be part way effective. This can also mean that the wrong type of candle or candle dressing was used.

What if the glass cracks?

If the candle is being used for self protection, this means that the candle broke the negativity in the environment. This can also mean witchcraft or the presence of secret enemies. If the candle is being used to dominate an individual, it means that the protection of the individual was broken.

What if the candle flame crackles?

If the flame on a candle makes a crackling noise, and the candle is for self protection, it means that someone is talking about you and has bad intentions directed toward you. If it is being used to harm an individual, this means that the individual is thinking about you.

What if the candle has more than one flame?

The center or main flame represents you. If the candle is being used for self protection, this means that each flame other than the center one represents an enemy. If the candle is being used to dominate another individual, this means that the individual is being helped by other people.

What if the candle flickers?

When a candle flickers, this signifies the presence of spirits.

What if the entire top of the candle including the wick is on fire?

If the entire top of the candle catches on fire, this means that the spell is being fought off by guardian spirits but more than likely, the spell will be successful.

What if the candle flame goes out in the middle of the spell?

If the spell is for self protection, this means that while you were performing the spell, witchcraft was directed your way and your spirits were unable to fight it off. If the spell was directed toward another individual, their spirits were able to fight the attack off and has alarmed the individual. Another type of spell must be performed.

Can a candle be extinguished and lit again later?

Only a candle being used to bring prosperity or success to an individual may be extinguished before it has completely burned. If the candle is being used to dominate or cause harm to another individual, the candle flame must never be put out because the spell will not work. In this case, the guardian spirits of the other individual will have time to prepare and reverse it back to you.

How do I put a candle flame out?

Candles can only be turned off by placing a plate over the top of the candle, thus allowing the flame to extinguise itself naturally. Candle flames can also be extinguished by using a candle snuffer.

What if I extinguished a candle and it later turned itself back on?

This means that your guardian spirits do not want you to turn the candle off beacuse they are detecting something good or bad for you. At any rate, if the candle is turned off they can not assist you effectively.

What if a seven day candle burns out before seven days?

If a 7 Day Candle burns out before seven days, this means that the spell is working fast and another one must be lighted immediataly. In the case of prosperity spells, this means money. In the case of reverse spells, this means that there is a lot of negativity around you. In the case of spell of harm, this means that the individuals spirit is fighting it off, but the spell will soon be effective.

What will make a candle spell work more effectively?

The use of the appropriate incense, floor wash or spiritual herbal bath are all ways to enhance a magical candle spell.

9

CANDLE
DRESSINGS
& SPELLS

Candle dressings are used in a variety of magic candle spells. The most effective and powerful candle dressings consist of an oil and herbal mixture. Every candle dressing is specially prepared for a unique circumstance and purpose. I have found that the following candle dressings are fast and effective. A candle should never be burned without it. The candle dressings are usually applied to 7 day glass religious candles.

THE FOLLOWING IS THE GENERAL FORMULA
FOR PREPARING CANDLE DRESSINGS

- *Add all of the herbs, powders and oils to 1 cup of Olive Oil*
- *Mix all of the ingredients well.*
- *Place the mixture in a storage jar until ready to use.*
- *Use 1 tablespoon of the mixture when dressing candle.*

ABBREVIATIONS USED IN THE FOLLOWING RECIPES:

TBSP. - *Tablespoon*   PWDR. - *Powder*   PWDRD. - *Powdered*

SEVEN AFRICAN POWERS
CANDLE DRESSING #1
BASE OIL
1 TBSP. ACHE DE SANTO (HERB)
1 TBSP. SHREDDED COCONUT
1 TBSP. VIOLET FLOWERS
2 TBSP. 7 AFRICAN POWERS OIL
1 TBSP. RED PRECIPITATE PWDR.

SEVEN AFRICAN POWERS
CANDLE DRESSING #2
BASE OIL
1 TBSP. ABRE CAMINO HERB
1 TBSP. PEPPERMINT LEAVES
1 TBSP. CINNAMON POWDER
1 TBSP. LILAC FLOWERS
2 TBSP. 7 AFRICAN POWERS OIL
1 TBSP. RED PRECIPITATE PWDR.

ELEGGUA CANDLE DRESSING
BASE OIL
1 TBSP. PWDRD. COCONUT
1 TBSP. PWDRD. ABRE CAMINO
1 TBSP. PWDRD. PALO DE GUAYABA
2 TBSP. ELEGGUA OPPORTUNITY OIL
1 TBSP. WHITE PRECIPITATE PWDR.

YEMAYA CANDLE DRESSING
BASE OIL
1 TBSP. ANIL POWDER
1 TBSP. COCONUT OIL
2 TBSP. YEMAYA PROTECTION OIL
7 DROPS VIOLET OIL
1 TBSP. WHITE PRECIPITATE PWDR.

OCHUN CANDLE DRESSING
BASE OIL
1 TBSP. CINNAMON POWDER
1 TBSP. CRUSHED ALMONDS
1 TBSP. DRIED ROSES
2 TBSP. OCHUN LOVE OIL
1 TBSP. YELLOW PRECIPITATE PWDR.

CHANGO CANDLE DRESSING
BASE OIL
1 TBSP. CLOVE POWDER
1 TBSP. BULL HORN POWDER
1 TBSP. MANDRAKE ROOT POWDER
2 TBSP. CHANGO DOMINATION OIL
1 TBSP. RED PRECIPITATE PWDR.

OBATALA
CANDLE DRESSING
BASE OIL
1 TBSP. VIOLET FLOWERS
1 TBSP. WHITE ROSES
1 TBSP. CASCARILLA PWDR.
2 TBSP. OBATALA PEACE OIL
1 TBSP. WHITE PRECIP. PWDR.

OCHOSI
CANDLE DRESSING
BASE OIL
1 TBSP. PWDRD. ABRE CAMINO
1 TBSP. DEER HORN PWDR.
1 TBLSP. ANIS
2 TBSP. OCHOSI PROTECTION OIL
1 TBSP. RED PRECIP. POWDER

OGGUN CANDLE DRESSING
BASE OIL
1 TBSP. PROTECTION POWDER
1 TBSP. SAGE
1 TBSP. EUCALYPTUS
2 TBSP. OGGUN GET AWAY OIL
1 TBSP. RED PRECIP. PWDR.

BABALU AYE
CANDLE DRESSING
BASE OIL
2 TBSP. DRY WHITE RICE
1 TBSP. RUE
2 TBSP. BABALU AYE HEALING OIL
1 TBSP. WHITE PRECIP. PWDR.

OZAIN CANDLE DRESSING
BASE OIL
1 TBSP. PWDRD. PALO VENCE BATALLA
1 TBSP. PWDRD. PALO COCUYO
1 TBSP. PWDRD. PALO ABRE CAMINO
2 TBSP. OZAIN SPIRIT OIL
1 TBSP. RED PRECIP. PWDR.

ORUNLA CANDLE DRESSING
BASE OIL
1 TBSP. ACHE DE SANTO HERB
1 TBSP. ABRE CAMINO HERB
1 TBSP. SANDLEWOOD POWDER
2 TBSP. ORUNLA DIVINATION OIL
1 TBSP. WHITE PRECIP. PWDR.

ZODIAC CANDLE DRESSINGS

AQUARIUS CANDLE DRESSING
BASE OIL
1 TBSP. PINE NEEDLES
1 TBSP. PEPPERMINT LEAVES
1 TBSP. LAVENDER FLOWERS
2 TBSP. AQUARIUS OIL
1 TBSP. WHITE PRECIP. PWDR.

LIBRA CANDLE DRESSING
BASE OIL
1 TBSP. ROSE FLOWERS
1 TBSP. SPEARMINT LEAVES
1 TBSP. ABRE CAMINO
2 TBSP. LIBRA OIL
1 TBSP. WHITE PRECIP. PWDR.

ARIES CANDLE DRESSING
BASE OIL
1 TBSP. CARNATION FLOWERS
1 TBSP. CINNAMON POWDER
1 TBSP. ALLSPICE POWDER
2 TBSP. ARIES OIL
1 TBSP. WHITE PRECIP. PWDR.

CANCER CANDLE DRESSING
BASE OIL
1 TBSP. ROSE FLOWERS
1 TBSP. LILAC FLOWERS
1 TBSP. GARDENIA FLOWERS
2 TBSP. CANCER OIL
1 TBSP. WHITE PRECIP. PWDR.

GEMINI CANDLE DRESSING
BASE OIL
1 TBSP. PEPPERMINT LEAVES
1 TBSP. ANIS
3 TBSP. GEMINI OIL
1 TBSP. WHITE PRECIP. PWDR.

CAPRICORN CANDLE DRESSING
BASE OIL
1 TBSP. PATCHOULY HERB
1 TBSP. HONEYSUCKLE FLOWERS
2 TBSP. CAPRICORN OIL
1 TBSP. WHITE PRECIP. POWDER

LEO CANDLE DRESSING
BASE OIL
1 TBSP. ROSEMARY LEAVES
1 TBSP. NUTMEG POWDER
1 TBSP. CINNAMON POWDER
2 TBSP. LEO OIL
1 TBSP. RED PRECIP. PWDR.

PISCES CANDLE DRESSING
BASE OIL
1 TBSP. NUTMEG POWDER
1 TBSP. LEMON LEAVES
1 TBSP. SANDALWOOD POWDER
2 TBSP. PISCES OIL
1 TBSP. WHITE PRECIP. PWDR.

SAGITTARIUS CANDLE DRESSING
BASE OIL
1 TBSP. ORANGE FLOWERS
1 TBSP. CARNATION FLOWERS
1 TBSP. GINGER ROOT
2 TBSP. SAGITTARIUS OIL
1 TBSP. WHITE PRECIP. PWDR.

TAURUS CANDLE DRESSING
BASE OIL
1 TBSP. VIOLET FLOWERS
1 TBSP. LILAC FLOWERS
1 TBSP. DAISY FLOWERS
2 TBSP. TAURUS OIL
1 TBSP. WHITE PRECIP. PWDR.

VIRGO CANDLE DRESSING
BASE OIL
1 TBSP. LAVENDER FLOWERS
1TBSP. PEPPERMINT LEAVES
1 TBSP. CRUSHED ALMONDS
2 TBSP. VIRGO OIL
1 TBSP. WHITE PRECIP. POWDER

SCORPIO CANDLE DRESSING
BASE OIL
1 TBSP. GINGER ROOT
1 TBSP. VANILLA EXTRACT
1 TBSP. VIOLET FLOWERS
2 TBSP. SCORPIO OIL
1 TBSP. WHITE PRECIP. PWDR.

COME TO ME
CANDLE DRESSING
BASE OIL
1 TBSP. PWDRD. PALO VEN A MI
1 TBSP. PWDRD. PALO AMANSA GUAPO
1 TBSP. PWDRD. PALO ABRE CAMINO
15 DROPS CINNAMON OIL
1 TBSP. RED PRECIPITAE POWDER

DRAGON'S BLOOD
CANDLE DRESSING
BASE OIL
1 TBSP. PWDRD. PALO NEGRO
1 TBSP. PWDRD. PALO AMARGO
1 TBSP. PWDRD. JINA
10 DROPS DRAGON'S BLOOD OIL
1 TBSP. RED PRECIP. POWDER

UNCROSSING
CANDLE DRESSING
BASE OIL
1 TBSP. PWDRD. PALO JABON
1 TBSP. PWDRD. PALO AMARGO
1 TBSP. PWDRD. PALO GUASIMO
5 DROPS SAGE OIL
10 DROPS RUE OIL
1 TBSP. WHITE PRECIP. PWDR.

MONEY DRAWING
CANDLE DRESSING
BASE OIL
1 TBSP. POWDERED PALO ABRE CAMINO
1 TBSP. POWDERED PALO DULCE
1 TBSP. WHITE RICE
10 DROPS PATCHOULY OIL
10 DROPS CINNAMON OIL
1 TBSP. RED PRECIPITATE POWDER

GAMBLER'S CANDLE DRESSING
BASE OIL
1 TBSP. ABRE CAMINO HERB
1 TBSP. POWDERED PALO RAMON
1 TBSP. POWDERED DEER HORN POWDER
10 DROPS ROSE OF JERICO OIL
7 DROPS COCONUT OIL
3 DROPS CINNAMON OIL
1 TBSP. RED PRECIPITATE POWDER

JOHN THE CONQUEROR
CANDLE DRESSING
BASE OIL
1 TBSP. PWDRD. HIGH JOHN THE CONQUEROR ROOTS
1 TBSP. BROWN MUSTARD SEEDS
1 TBSP. PATCHOULY POWDER
1 TBSP. FRESH MINT LEAVES
10 DROPS VANILLA OIL
1 TBSP. RED PRECIP. POWDER

PALO MAYOMBE DESTRUCTION
CANDLE DRESSING #1
BASE OIL (USED CAR MOTOR OIL)
1 TBSP. BLACK PEPPER
1 TBSP. PWDRD. PALO CAMBIA RUMBA
1 TBSP. POWDERED HUMAN BONE
(SKULL)
1 TBSP. POWDERED PALO BOMBA
1 TBSP. POWDERED PALO TORCIDO
1 TBSP. POWDERED PALO MUERTO
1 TBSP. RED PRECIP. POWDER

PALO MAYOMBE DESTRUCTION
CANDLE DRESSING #2
BASE OIL (USED CAR MOTOR OIL)
1 TBSP. POWDERED PALO PINO
1 TBSP. POWDERES GUAYABA
1 TBSP. PWDRD. PALO MUERTO
1 TBSP. CEMETERY DIRT
1 TBSP. PWDRD. HUMAN BONE
(HANDS AND FEET)
1 TBSP. BLACK PEPPER
1 TBSP. BLACK DOG HAIR
1 TBSP. BLACK PRECIP. PWDR.

PALO MAYOMBE LOVE
CANDLE DRESSING
BASE OIL
1 TBSP. PWDRD. PALO JERINGA
1 TBSP. PWDRD. PALO AMANSA GUAPO
1 TBSP. PWDRD PALO ABRE CAMINO
1 TBSP. PWDRD HUMAN BONE
(BOTH HANDS)
1 TBSP. HUMINGBIRD FEATHERS
1 TBSP. RED PRECIP. POWDER

PALO MAYOMBRE DOMINATION
CANDLE DRESSING
BASE OIL
1 TBSP. PWDRD. PALO CAMBIA VOZ
1 TBSP. PWDRD. PALO SANTO
1 TBSP. PWDRD. PALO CAMITO
1 TBSP. PWDRD. SPIDERS
10 DROPS SNAKE OIL
1 TBSP. PWDRD. HUMAN BONE *(BOTH HANDS)*
1 TBSP. RED PRECIPITATE POWDER

PALO MAYOMBE
ESCAPE THE LAW &
COURT VICTORY
CANDLE DRESSING
BASE OIL
1 TBSP. PWDRD. PALO ABRE CAMINO
1 TBSP. PWDRD. PALO AMARGO
1 TBSP. PWDRD. PALO JOBOVAN
1 TBSP. PWDRD. PALO JUSTICIA
1 TBSP. PWDRD. PALO ESPANTA POLICIA
1 TBSP. PWDRD. PALO NEGRO
1 TBSP. PWDRD. HUMAN BONE *(BOTH FEET)*
1 TBSP. DEER HORN POWDER
1 TBSP. RED PRECIP. POWDER

PALO MAYOMBE FAST LUCK
CANDLE DRESSING
BASE OIL
2 TBSP. PWDRD. PALO AMARGO
1 TBSP. PWDRD. PALO ABRE CAMINO
1 TBSP. PWDRD. PALO GUAYABA
1 TBSP. PWDRD. PALO NEGRO
1 TBSP. DEER HORN POWDER
1 TBSP. PWDRD. HUMAN BONES *(HANDS)*
1 TBSP. RED PRECIPITATE POWDER

PALO MAYOMBE REVERSE CANDLE DRESSING
BASE OIL
1 TBSP. PWDRD. PALO CABALERRO
1 TBSP. PWDRD. PALO CANPECHE
1 TBSP. PWDRD. PALO GUAYABA
1 TBSP. PWDRD. PALO ESPANTA MUERTO
1 TBSP. POWDERED HUMAN BONE *(HANDS)*
1 TBSP. KOSHER ROCK SALT
1 TBSP. POWDERED BLACK DOG BONE *(HEAD AND LEGS)*
1 TBSP. WHITE PRECIPITATE POWDER
1 TBSP. RED PRECIPITATE POWDER

EASY 7 DAY CANDLE SPELLS

FAST MONEY SPELL
GREEN CANDLE
SEVEN AFRICAN POWERS
CANDLE DRESSING #1
LIGHT THE CANDLE FOR 7 DAYS

FAST LUCK SPELL
SEVEN COLORED CANDLE
SEVEN AFRICAN POWERS
CANDLE DRESSING #2
LIGHT THE CANDLE FOR 21 DAYS

FAST LOVE SPELL
YELLOW CANDLE
OCHUN CANDLE DRESSING
LIGHT THE CANDLE FOR 7 DAYS

FAST JOB SPELL
WHITE CANDLE
ELEGGUA CANDLE DRESSING
LIGHT THE CANDLE FOR 21 DAYS

TO BREAK A SPELL
REVERSE BLACK / RED CANDLE
ELEGGUA CANDLE DRESSING
LIGHT THE CANDLE FOR 21 DAYS

DOMINATE AN INDIVIDUAL
RED CANDLE
CHANGO CANDLE DRESSING
LIGHT THE CANDLE FOR 14 DAYS

TO BRING DEVINE JUSTICE
RUN DEVIL RUN CANDLE
PALO MAYOMBE REVERSE
CANDLE DRESSING
LIGHT THE CANDLE FOR 14 DAYS

TO BRING SPIRITUAL
COMMUNICATION
GREEN / YELLOW CANDLE
ORUNLA CANDLE DRESSING
LIGHT THE CANDLE FOR 7 DAYS

TO WIN A COURT CASE
THE JUST JUDGE CANDLE
OCHOSI CANDLE DRESSING
LIGHT THE CANDLE 7 DAYS
BEFORE GOING TO COURT

TO SEPARATE INDIVIDUALS
BLACK CANDLE
PALO MAYOMBE DESTRUCTION
CANDLE DRESSING #1
LIGHT THE CANDLE FOR 21 DAYS

TO REVERSE WITCHCRAFT
BLACK / RED CANDLE
QUICK REVERSE CANDLE DRESSING
LIGHT THE CANDLE FOR 7 DAYS

TO BRING ON A WEDDING
ADAM AND EVE CANDLE
COME TO ME CANDLE DRESSING
LIGHT THE CANDLE FOR 21 DAYS

TO BRING PEACE TO A HOME
PEACEFUL HOME CANDLE
YEMAYA CANDLE DRESSING
LIGHT THE CANDLE FOR 7 DAYS

TO BRING MONEY
GREEN / YELLOW CANDLE
MONEY DRAWING
CANDLE DRESSING
LIGHT THE CANDLE FOR 7 DAYS

BRING A GAMBLER LUCK
HIGH JOHN THE CONQ.
CANDLE DRESSING
LIGHT THE CANDLE FOR 21 DAYS

TO DISPELL EVIL SPIRITS
SAN MIGUEL ARCHANGEL CANDLE
PALO MAYOMBE REVERSE
CANDLE DRESSING
LIGHT THE CANDLE FOR 21 DAYS

TO FIND OUT YOUR
SECRET ENEMIES
SANTA BARBARA CANDLE
OCHOSI CANDLE DRESSING
LIGHT THE CANDLE FOR 21 DAYS

BRING YOUR GUARDIAN
ANGEL CLOSER TO YOU
WHITE CANDLE
OBATALA CANDLE DRESSING
LIGHT THE CANDLE FOR 7 DAYS

TO FIND A JOB
SAN SIMON GREEN / YELLOW CANDLE
ZODIAC CANDLE DRSNG (YOUR SIGN)
MONEY DRAWING CANDLE DRESSING
LIGHT THE CANDLE FOR 21 DAYS

TO REUNITE LOVERS
HUMMINGBIRD CANDLE
PALO MAYOMBE LOVE CANDLE DRSNG
LIGHT THE CANDLE FOR 21 DAYS

QUICK UNCROSSING SPELL
UNCROSSING CANDLE
DRAGON'S BLOOD CANDLE DRSNG
LIGHT THE CANDLE FOR 14 DAYS

TO STOP GOSSIPING
TAPA BOCA CANDLE
PALO MAYOMBE DESTRUCTION OIL #2
LIGHT THE CANDLE FOR 21 DAYS

TO CONQUEROR OBSTACLES
SANTO NINO ATOCHA CANDLE
PALO MAYOMBE FAST LUCK
 CANDLE DRESSING
LIGHT THE CANDLE FOR 14 DAYS

TO CONQUER YOUR ENEMIES
CONGO MACHO CANDLE
JOHN THE CONQUEROR
 CANDLE DRESSING
LIGHT THE CANDLE FOR 21 DAYS

TO BREAK A SPELL
SPELL BREAKER CANDLE
OBATALA CANDLE DRESSING
LIGHT THE CANDLE FOR 14 DAYS

GET RID OF UNWANTED PEOPLE
RETIRE CANDLE
PALO MAYOMBE DESTRUCTION
 CANDLE DRESSING
LIGHT THE CANDLE FOR 21 DAYS

TO KEEP YOUR JOB
GOLD CANDLE
MONEY DRAWING CANDLE DRSNG.
LIGHT THE CANDLE FOR 21 DAYS

FAST HEALING
PURPLE CANDLE
OBATALA CANDLE DRESSING
LIGHT THE CANDLE FOR 21 DAYS

OPEN YOUR ROADS TO SUCCESS
SEVEN AFRICAN POWERS CANDLE
SEVEN AFRICAN POWERS
CANDLE DRESSING #2
LIGHT THE CANDLE FOR 21 DAYS

BRING A WOMAN FERTILITY
THE VIRGIN OF REGLA CANDLE
YEMAYA CANDLE DRESSING
LIGHT THE CANDE FOR 21 DAYS

BRING A LOVER TO YOU
YELLOW / RED CANDLE
CHANGO CANDLE DRESSING
LIGHT THE CANDLE FOR 21 DAYS

TO JINX AN INDIVIDUAL
BLOCK BUSTER CANDLE
PALO MAYOMBE DESTRUCTION
CANDLE DRESSING #1
LIGHT THE CANDLE FOR 21 DAYS

TO DESTROY AN INDIVIDUAL
BLACK CANDLE
PALO MAYOMBE DESTRUCTION
CANDLE DRESSING #1
LIGHT THE CANDLE FOR 21 DAYS

TO RELEASE AN INDIVIDUAL FROM JAIL
COURT CASE CANDLE
PALO MAYOMBE ESCAPE THE LAW
CANDLE DRESSING
LIGHT THE CANDLE FOR 21 DAYS

TO PACIFY YOUR ENEMIES
AJO MACHO CANDLE
CHANGO CANDLE DRESSING
BALSAMO TRANQUILO OIL
LIGHT THE CANDLE FOR 21 DAYS

TO MAKE YOUR ENEMIES RESTLESS
RED CANDLE
OZAIN CANDLE DRESSING
LIGHT THE CANDLE FOR 21 DAYS

TO FIND AN ITEM LOST
SAN ANTONIO CANDLE
ELEGGUA CANDLE DRESSING
LIGHT THE CANDLE FOR 7 DAYS

10

TALLOW CANDLES

VELAS DE CEBO

Tallow candles can be used in a variety of magical spells. The use of these candles is common in the practice of magic in Mexico and Central America. Because the candles are extremely delicate and soft, they can be prepared (dressed) with a multitude of ingredients which will help a spell work faster. In general, lard candles are prepared with dry candle dressings because they stick to the soft surface of the lard candles. The following is the general formula how to prepare all lard candles.

GENERAL FORMULA FOR PREPARING TALLOW CANDLES

• *Carefully roll the candle in the appropiate ingredient.*
• *Place the prepared lard candle in a plastic storage container.*
• *Place the storage container in the freezer until ready to use.*

GENERAL FORMULA FOR PREPARING DRY CANDLE DRESSING

• *Mix all of the ingredients together.*
• *Place the mixture in a glass storage jar until ready to use.*

LOVE DRESSING
1 TBLSP. CINNAMON POWDER
1 TBLSP. PWDRD. PALO AMANSA GUAPO
1 TBLSP. PWDRD. PALO VEN A MI
1 TBLSP. DRIED ROSES
1 TBLSP. DRIED LILACS
1 TBLSP. HUMMINGBIRD POWDER

MONEY DRESSING
1 TBLSP. PWDRD.
   PALO ABRE CAMINO
1 TBLSP. PWDRD. PALO GUAYABA
1 TBLSP. PWDRD. PALO NAMO
1 TBLSP. MAGNETIC SAND
1 TBLSP. CINNAMON POWDER

PROSPERITY DRESSING
1 TBLSP. ABRE CAMINO HERB
1 TBLSP. CRUSHED ALMONDS
1 TBLSP. PATCHOULY POWDER
1 TBLSP. BOTON DE ORO HERB
1 TBLSP. NUTMEG POWDER

GAMBLER'S DRESSING
1 TBLSP. DRIED PEPPERMINT
1 TBLSP. PWDRD.
   HIGH JOHN THE CONQUEROR
1 TBLSP. CINNAMON POWDER
1 TBLSP. DRIED PARSELY
1 TBLSP. DEERHORN POWDER

DOMINATION DRESSING #1 (LOVE)
1 TBLSP. CLOVE POWDER
2 TBLSP. CINNAMON POWDER
1 TBLSP. DRIED PEPPERMINT
1 TBLSP. PWDRD. PALO MULATTO
1 TBLSP. PWDRD.
   PALO AMANSA GUAPO

DOMINATION DRESSING #2 (DESTRUCTION)
1 TBLSP. PWDRD. PALO VENCE BATALLA
1 TBLSP. BULLHORN POWDER
1 TBLSP. CRUSHED GLASS
1 TBLSP. PWDRD. PALO MUERTO
1 TBLSP. PWDRD. CAMBIA RUMBA

DESTRUCTION DRESSING
1 TBLSP. PWDRD. PALO BOMBA
1 TBLSP.SNAKE POWDER
1 TBLSP. BLACK SALT
1 TBLSP. CEMETERY DIRT
1 TBLSP. PWDRD. HUMAN BONE
   (HANDS)

CONFLICT DRESSING
1 TBLSP. PWDRD. CAMBIA RUMBA
1 TBLSP. PWDRD. PALO TORCIDO
1 OZ. BLACK CAT FUR
1 OZ. BLACK DOG FUR
1 TBLSP. PWDRD. BAT

COURT VICTORY DRESSING
1 TBLSP. DEERHORN POWDER
1 TBLSP. PWDRD. PALO ABRE CAMINO
1 TBLSP. PWDRD. PALO AMARGO
1 TBLSP. PWDRD. PALO NEGRO
2 TBLSP. PWDRD. PALO ESPANTA
   POLICIA

TAPA BOCA DRESSING (SHUT YOUR MOUTH)
1 TBLSP. PWDRD. PALO CAMBIA VOZ
1 TBLSP. PWDRD. PALO AMARGO
1 TBLSP. PWDRD. PALO SANTO
1 TBLSP. PWDRD. PALO ESPUELDE
   GALLO
2 TBLSP. AFRICAN FROG PWDR.

DO AS I SAY DRESSING
1 TBLSP. PWDRD. PALO CAMBIA VIZ
1 TBLSP. PWDRD. PALO DULCE
1 TBLSP. PWDRD. PALO DIABLO
2 TBLSP. SNAKE PWDR.

ATTRACTION DRESSING
1 TBLSP. PWDRD. PALO PARA MI
1 TBLSP. PWDRD. PALO VEN A MI
1 TBLSP. PWDRD.
   PALO AMANSA GUAPO
1 TBLSP. MAGNETIC SAND
1 TBLSP. SNAKE POWDER

CONQUER YOUR ENEMIES
1 TBLSP. PWDRD. PALO VENCE
   BATALLA
1 TBLSP. PWDRD. HIGH JOHN THE
   CONQUEROR ROOT
1 TBLSP. PWDRD. PALO CABALLERO
2 TBLSP. DRAGON'S BLOOD PWDR.

GET AWAY DRESSING
2 TBLSP. DEERHORN POWDER
1 TBLSP. PWDRD. PALO ABRE CAMINO
1 TBLSP. EGGSHELL POWDER
1 TBLSP. NUTMEG POWDER

SPIRITUAL CLEANSING
1 TBLSP. PWDRD. PALO JOBON
1 TBLSP. PWDRD. PALO CLAVO
1 TBLSP. PWDRD. PALO CANPECHE
2 TBLSP. EGGSHELL POWDER
1 TBLSP. DRAGON'S BLOOD POWDER

MONEY DRAWING DRESSING
1 TBLSP. ALLSPICE
1 TBLSP. ANISE
1 TBLSP. PWDRD. PALO DULCE
1 TBLSP. PWDRD. PALO HUESO
1 TBLSP. PWDRD.
  ROSE OF JERICO HERB

SEPARATION DRESSING
1 TBLSP. PWDRD. PALO MUERTO
1 TBLSP. PWDRD. PALO CAMBIA RUMBA
1 TBLSP. PALO UNA DE GATO
1 TBLSP. CRUSHED GLASS
1 TBLSP. BLACK PEPPER
1 TBLSP. RED CHILE PEPPER PWDR.

REVERSIBLE DRESSING
1 TBLSP. RED PRECIPITATE PWDR.
2 TBLSP. WHITE PRECIPITATE PWDR.
2 TBLSP. PWDRD. PALO ESPANTA
MUERTO
1 TBLSP. DRAGON'S BLOOD POWDER

DIVINE JUSTICE DRESSING
2 TBLSP. PWDRD. PALO GUAYABA
1 TBLSP. PWDRD. PALO JUSTICA
1 TBLSP. PWDRD. PALO VENCE BATALLA
1 TBLSP. DEERHORN POWDER

HOT FOOT DRESSING
2 TBLSP. BLACK PEPPER
2 TBLSP. PICA PICA
2 TBLSP. RED CHILE PEPPER POWDER
1 TBLSP. PWDRD. PALO DIABLO

HEALING DRESSING
2 TBLSP. CRSHD. EUCALYPTUS LEAVES
1 TABLESPOON SAGE
1 TBLSP. KOSHER ROCK SALT
1 TBLSP. PWDRD. PALO CLAVO
1 TBLSP. EGGSHELL POWDER

TO SEPARATE INDIVIDUALS

INGREDIENTS

1. Separation Candle Dressing
2. Black Pepper Oil
3. Pica Pica Powder
4. Three Black Tallow Candles

PREPARATION

1. Write one of the individuals name nine times on a piece of brown paper. Write the other individuals name nine times on the same paper. The names should cross each other in the form of a cross.
2. Anoint the candle with the Black Pepper Oil.
3. Roll each of candles in the candle dressing.
4. Place the paper into the center of a white plate.
5. Sprinkle the Pica Pica over the names.
6. Place one candle in the center of the paper and then light.
7. Light one candle a day for three consecutive days.
8. After the third candle has completely burned, wrap the remaining ingredients in a black cloth and drop it near the individuals home.

TO BRING PROSPERITY

INGREDIENTS

1. Prosperity Candle Dressing
2. Seven Green Tallow Candles

PREPARATION

1. Roll each of the tallow candles in the candle dressing.
2. Write your name seven times on a brown piece of paper.
3. Place the paper in the center of a white plate.
4. Place one candle in the center of the paper.
5. Light the candle and recite a prayer to the Seven African Powers.
6. Light one candle for seven consecutive days.

This spell should be started on a Monday morning.

TO BRING AN INDIVIDUAL A JOB

INGREDIENTS

1. *Money Candle Dressing*
2. *Yang Ylang Oil*
3. *Three White Tallow Candles*

PREPARATION

1. *Anoint each of candles with Ylang Ylang Oil.*
2. *Roll each of the candles in the candle dressing.*
3. *Place your picture in the center of a white plate.*
4. *Place the candles around the picture.*
5. *Light the candles and recite a prayer to Eleggua and ask him to open the doors to opportunity.*

This spell should be performed on Mondays.

TO ATTRACT LOVE

INGREDIENTS

1. *Attraction Candle Dressing*
2. *Ochun Love Oil*
3. *Zodiac Oil (Your Sign)*
4. *Honey*
5. *Five Fishing Hooks*
6. *Cinnamon Powder*
7. *Five Red Lard Candles*

PREPARATION

1. *Anoint the candles with the Ochun Love Oil and the Zodiac Oil.*
2. *Roll each of candles in the candle dressing.*
3. *Write your name five times on a piece of brown paper.*
4. *Insert the five fishing hooks through the paper.*
5. *Place the paper into the center of a white plate.*
6. *Pour the honey over the paper.*
7. *Sprinkle the cinnamon on the honey.*
8. *Place one of the candles in the center of the honey mixture.*
9. *Light the candle and recite a prayer to Ochun.*
10. *Light one candle each day for five consecutive days.*
11. *On the 6th day, take the remaining ingredients on the plate leave it on a river bank.*

TO DOMINATE A LOVER

INGREDIENTS

1. Domination Candle Dressing #1
2. Ambergris Oil
3. Hisbiscus Oil
4. Six Red Tallow Candles

PREPARATION

1. Anoint each of the candles with the Ambergris and Hibiscus Oils.
2. Roll each of the candles in the candle dressing.
3. Write your name six times over the picture of the desired individual.
4. Place the photo in the center of a white plate.
5. Light one candle in the center of the photo and recite a prayer to Chango.
6. Light one candle each day for six consecutive days.
7. On the 7th day, wrap the plate in a red cloth and leave in a wooded area or field with six pennies.

TO DOMINATE AN INDIVIDUAL

INGREDIENTS

1. Destruction Candle Dressing
2. Used Car Oil
3. Cemetery Dirt
4. Nine Black Tallow Candles

PREPARATION

1. Anoint each of the candles with the used car oil.
2. Roll each of the candles in the candle dressing.
3. Write the name of the individual nine times on a brown piece of paper.
4. Place the paper in the center of a white plate.
5. Sprinkle the cemetery dirt over the paper. The name should be completely covered.
6. Place all of the candles in a circle around the dirt mixture.
7. Light one candle each hour for nine consecutive hours.
8. Each time you light a candle, recite the prayer of the Intranquil Spirits.
9. When the last of the candles has completely burned out, wrap the plate in a black cloth and leave it in a cemetery along with nine pennies.

TO DESTROY AN ENEMY

INGREDIENTS

1. Domination Candle Dressing #2
2. Destruction Candle Dressing
3. One Black Cloth Voodoo Doll
4. Scorpion Powder
5. African Frog Powder
6. Eighty - One Straight Pins
7. Nine Black Candles

PREPARATION

1. Mix both candle dressings together with the Scorpion and African Frog powders.
2. Roll each of the candles in the above mixture.
3. Write the individuals name nine times on a piece of brown paper.
4. Insert the paper into the stomach of the Voodoo Doll.
5. Place the doll on a white plate.
6. Place all of the candles in the form of a circle around the doll on the plate.
7. Light one candle and recite a prayer to the Intranquil Spirits.
8. Pierce the doll with nine pins as you recite the prayer.
9. Light one candle each day for nine consecutive days. Nine pins should be stuck into the doll each day.
10. After the 9th candle has completely burned, take the doll to a cemetery and bury over a grave.

COURT VICTORY SPELL

INGREDIENTS

1. Court Victory Candle Dressing
2. Anise Oil
3. Deerhorn Powder
4. Seven White Tallow Candles

PREPARATION

1. Anoint each of the candles with the oil.
2. Roll all of the candles in the candle dressing.
3. Light one candle each day for seven consecutive days.
4. Each time you light a candle, recite a prayer to the Orisha Ochosi and the Just Judge.
5. On the day of court, sprinkle a small amount of deerhorn powder on the courtroom floor.

This spell should be performed seven days prior to the court hearing.

TO REVERSE THE EVIL EYE

INGREDIENTS

1. Reversible Candle Dressing   *3. Reversible Oil*
2. Coconut Oil   *4. Seven White Tallow Candles*

PREPARATION

1. Anoint the candles with the coconut and reversible oils.
2. Roll all of the candles in the candle dressing.
3. Place your photo in the center of a white plate.
4. Place one candle in the center of the photo.
5. Light one candle each day for seven consecutive days.
6. Recite a prayer to Eleggua each time you light a candle.
7. On the 8th day, wrap the plate in a white cloth and leave it by a crossroads along with 21 pennies.

TO RETURN A LOVER

INGREDIENTS

1. Love Candle Dressing   *3. Cinnamon Oil*
2. Ambergris Oil   *4. Twenty-One Red Tallow Candles*

PREPARATION

1. Anoint each of the candles with the Ambergis and Cinnamon oils.
2. Roll each of the candles in the candle dressing.
3. Write your name across the individual's picture twenty-one times.
4. Place the picture in the center of a white plate.
5. Place one of the candles in the center of the picture.
6. Light the candle and recite a prayer to Eleggua.
7. Light one candle a day for twenty-one consecutive days.

When the last candle has completely burned, wrap the plate and the contents in a red cloth and bury near your front door. Place 21 pennies in the hole before covering over with the dirt.

TO BRING PEACE TO A HOME

INGREDIENTS

1. Anil Powder
2. Sea Salt
3. Eggshell Powder
4. Almond Oil
5. Seven White Tallow Candles

PREPARATION

1. Anoint the candles with the Almond Oil.
2. Mix the Anil and the Sea Salt together.
3. Roll the candles in the above mixture.
4. Light one candle each day for seven consecutive days.
5. Recite a prayer to Yemaya each day.

On the 7th day, take a Spiritual Bath consisting of 1 part coconut milk, 1 part Holy Water, 1 tablespoon of Anil and 1 cup Kosher Rock Salt.

TO STOP AN INDIVIDUAL FROM GOSSIPING

INGREDIENTS

1. Tapa Boca Candle Dressing
2. Pica Pica Powder
3. Black Pepper Oil
4. Black Cloth Voodoo Doll
5. Nine Pins
6. Nine Black Tallow Candles

PREPARATION

1. Write the individuals name nine times on a brown piece of paper. Write the individuals name nine more times . The two sets of names should intersect to form a cross.
2. Open the stomach of the doll and insert the paper. Sew the stomach up.
3. Pierce the nine pins through the mouth of the doll calling out the name of the individual nine times.
4. Wrap black thread around the mouth of the doll and tie.
5. Place the doll in the center of a white plate.
6. Anoint the candles in the oil.
7. Roll the candles in the Pica Pica and the Candle Dressing.

(Continued)

8. *Place all of the candles in the form of a circle around the doll.*
9. *Light one candle each hour for nine hours.*
10. *Recite a prayer to the Intraquil Spirits and say:* **As this candle dies so may your mouth die.**
11. *After the last candle has completely burned, hang the doll upside down from a tree in the cemetery.*

TO BRING DIVINE JUSTICE

INGREDIENTS

1. *Divine Justice Candle Dressing*
2. *Reverse Oil*
3. *Powdered Palo Vence Batalla*
4. *Seven White Tallow Candles*

PREPARATION

1. *Anoint the candles with the oil.*
2. *Roll all of the candles in the Candle Dressing and the powdered Palo Vence Batalla.*
3. *Place one of the candles in the center of a white plate.*
4. *Light the candle and recite a prayer to the Just Judge.*
5. *Light one candle each day for seven consecutive days.*

TO HEAL AN INDIVIDUAL FROM SICKNESS

INGREDIENTS

1. *Healing Candle Dressing*
2. *Coconut Oil*
3. *White Precipitate Powder*
4. *Seven White Tallow Candles*

PREPARATION

1. *Anoint the candles with the oil.*
2. *Roll all of the candles in the White Precipitate Powder and candle dressing.*
3. *Place the photo of the sick individual on a white plate.*
4. *Place one candle in the center of the photo .*
5. *Light the candle and recite a prayer to San Lazaro.*

(Continued)

6. Light one candle each hour for seven consecutive hours.

Allow the plate with the ingredients to remain in the individual's home for 7 days. On the 8th day, wrap the ingredients in a white cloth with seven pennies and leave it in a church.

TO MAKE A PERSON LEAVE

INGREDIENTS

1. Hot Foot Candle Dressing
2. Black Salt
3. Cemetery Dirt
4. Dirt from the Individual's Home
5. Six Black Tallow Candles

PREPARATION

1. Write the individuals name nine times on a piece of brown paper.
2. Place the paper into the center of a white plate.
3. Mix the candle dressing, Black Salt, Cemetery Dirt and the Dirt from the individuals home together.
4. Roll all of the candles in the mixture.
5. Place one of the candles in the center of the paper.
6. Light the candle and allow it to completely burn.
7. Light one candle each day for six consecutive days.

On the 7th day, leave the contents in a cemetery along with 9 pennies.

TO RECEIVE A RAISE IN SALARY

INGREDIENTS

1. Money Candle Dressing
2. Anis Seeds
3. Brown Mustard Seeds
4. Five Green Tallow Candles

PREPARATION

1. Write the name of your boss five times on a piece of brown paper. Write your name across their name five times. The name should intersect each other in the form of a cross.

2. *Place the paper in the center of a white plate.*
3. *Mix the candle dressing, Anis Seeds and the Brown Mustard Seeds together.*
4. *Roll all of the candles in the above mixture.*
5. *Place one candle in the center of the paper.*
6. *Light the candle and recite a prayer to the Seven African Powers.*
7. *Light one candle each day for five consecutive days.*

This spell should be started on Monday mornings.

TO MAKE SOMEONE GIVE YOU MONEY

INGREDIENTS

1. *Do As I Say Candle Dressing*
2. *Snake Oil*
3. *Red Precipitate Powder*
4. *Six Red Tallow Candles*

PREPARATION

1. *Take six pieces of brown paper and write the individuals name six times on each piece.*
2. *Wrap the paper around the candle and wrap with red thread. Do this with each of the six candles.*
3. *Anoint each of the candles with the oil.*
4. *Roll all of the candles in the candle dressing and the Red Precipitate Powder.*
5. *Place one of the candles on a white plate.*
6. *Light the candle and recite a prayer to Chango.*
7. *Light one candle each day for six consecutive days.*

On the 7th day, wrap the ingredients in a red cloth and dispose of it in a field with 6 pennies.

TO FIND YOUR HIDDEN ENEMIES

INGREDIENTS

1. Divine Justice Candle Dressing
2. Hot Foot Candle Dressing
3. Red Precipitate Powder
4. Ochosi Oil
5. Seven Red Tallow Candles

PREPARATION

1. Anoint all of the candles with the oil.
2. Roll the candles in both candle dressings and the Red Precipitate Powder.
3. Place one candle in the center of a white plate and then light.
4. Recite a prayer to Chango and ask him to reveal your enemies.
5. Light one candle each day for seven consecutive days.

On the 8th day place the contents in a brown paper bag and leave it at a crossroad with 6 pennies.

TO CALL THE DEAD

INGREDIENTS

1. Dirt Frown Seven Cemeteries
2. Powdered Palo Malambo
3. Powdered Palo Ramon
4. Powdered Human Bone (Skull)
5. Olive Oil
6. One White Tallow Candle

PREPARATION

1. Anoint the candle with the oil.
2. Mix all of the above ingredients together.
3. Roll the candle in the mixture.
4. Place a small mirror into the center of a white plate.
5. Place the candle in the center of the mirror.
6. Light the candle and invoke the spirits.

This spell should be done at 12 midnight.

The doorway to the spirits will be open for communication only as long as the candle is burning. This spell should be done on a Friday.

TO SEND A SPIRIT

INGREDIENTS

1. Bat Powder
2. Snake Powder
3. Black Dog Bone Powder
   (Legs and Head)
4. Black Cat Bone Powder
   (Legs and Head)

5. Human Bone Powder
   (Head, Legs, Hands)
6. Olive Oil
7. Nine White Tallow Candles

PREPARATION

1. Mix all of the powders together.
2. Anoint the candles with the oil.
3. Roll all of the candles in the powdered mixture.
4. Place one of the candles in the center of a white plate.
5. Light the candle and invoke the spirits with your request.
6. When the candle has completly burned, light another one.
7. Do until all of the candles have completly burned.

This spirit will manifest to do your request only as long as the candles are burning. This spell can only be done on a full moon. The spirit will be able to manifest as a **Black Cat, Black Dog** or in **Human Form.**

11

HANDMADE BEE'S WAX CANDLES

The art of making candles by hand is infact a very Old World tradition that dates back hundreds and even thousands of years. Making handmade candles can be quite an enjoyable event, although it might get a little messy. By making handmade candles, you will be able to add many magical ingredients that will enhance a magical ritual. Many of the following candles are in themselves complete spells. The following is the general formula for making Traditional Bee's Wax Candles.

THE GENERAL FORMULA FOR
MAKING BEE'S WAX CANDLES

* *Heat and boil 2 pounds of natural bee's wax in a metal pan.*
* *After the wax has melted, add all of the herbs and powders.*
* *Stir in all of the ingredients and mix well.*
* *Turn the heat off and allow the wax to remain for 10 minutes.*
* *After the 10 minutes, add in all of the oils.*
* *Mix all of the ingredients well.*
* *If desired, special candle colors can be added.*

• *Make sure cotton candle wick has been placed and anchored to glass bottom before pouring the wax into the container.*
• *7 Day Religious Glass Candle containers are best suited for this formula.*

ELEGGUA'S PROSPERITY CANDLE

HERBAL INGREDIENTS
1/2 CUP ABRE CAMINO
1/8 CUP BOTON DE ORO
1/8 CUP PARAISO
1/8 CUP SHREDDED COCONUT

ESSENTIAL OILS
30 DROPS COCONUT
30 DROPS PEPPERMINT
30 DROPS SASSAFRAS
30 DROPS ORRIS
30 DROPS ANISE

ELEGGUA'S REVERSE CANDLE

HERBAL INGREDIENTS
2 TBLSP. RED PRECIPITATE PWDR.
1/4 CUP COFFEE GROUNDS
1/8 CUP BLACK PEPPER
1 TABLESPOON PICA PICA

ESSENTIAL OILS
30 DROPS COCONUT
30 DROPS PEPPERMINT
60 DROPS AMBROSIA
30 DROPS COFFEE

OCHUN'S LOVE CANDLE

HERBAL INGREDIENTS
1/2 CUP CINNAMON STICKS
1/8 CUP CINNAMON POWDER
1/4 CUP YELLOW ROSE PETALS
1/8 CUP LILAC FLOWERS

ESSENTIAL OILS
30 DROPS CÍNNAMON
40 DROPS HONEY
30 DROPS AMBERGRIS
50 DROPS LILAC

YEMAYA'S PEACE CANDLE

HERBAL INGREDIENTS
1 TABLESPOON ANIL
1/8 CUP SEAWEED
1/2 CUP CHRYSANTHEMUM FLOWERS
1/4 CUP LILAC FLOWERS

ESSENTIAL OILS
40 DROPS CHRYSANTHEMUM
25 DROPS WATERMELON
25 DROPS LILAC
20 DROPS LAVANDER
40 DROPS HYACINTH

OCHOSI'S COURT VICTORY CANDLE

HERBAL INGREDIENTS
2 TBLSP. DEERHORN POWDER
1/4 CUP ANISE HERB
1/8 CUP DRAGON'S BLOOD POWDER
1/4 CUP HIGH JOHN
THE CONQUEROR ROOTS

ESSENTIAL OILS
30 DROPS ANGELICA
30 DROPS ANISE
30 DROPS DRAGON'S BLOOD
30 DROPS PINE
30 DROPS NUTMEG

CHANGO'S DOMINATION CANDLE

HERBAL INGREDIENTS
2 TABLESPOONS SANDALWOOD PWDR.
1/4 CUP HISBISCUS FLOWERS
2 TABLESPOONS CLOVE PWDR.
1/4 CUP PARAISO

ESSENTIAL OILS
30 DROPS CLOVE
30 DROPS HYSSOP
30 DROPS APPLE
30 DROPS CIVIT
30 DROPS VERTIVERT

OZAIN'S PROPHECY CANDLE

HERBAL INGREDIENTS
1/4 CUP MISLETOE HERB
1/4 CUP PEPPERMINT LEAVES

ESSENTIAL OILS
30 DROPS PEPPERMINT
30 DROPS YLANG YANG
30 DROPS MISTLETOE
30 DROPS EVERGREEN
30 DROPS ACACIA

OBATALA'S PURIFICATION CANDLE

HERBAL INGREDIENTS
1/8 CUP SHREDDED COCONUT
1/8 CUP EUCALYPTUS LEAVES
1/4 CUP RUE
1 TBLSP. CASCARILLA (EGGSHELL PWDR.)
1 TBLSP. WHITE PRECIPITATE PWDR.

ESSENTIAL OILS
60 DROPS COCONUT
30 DROPS EUCALYPTUS
30 DROPS RUE
30 DROPS ROSEMARY

SAN LAZARO'S HEALING CANDLE

HERBAL INGREDIENTS
1/4 CUP SAGE
1/8 CUP RUE
1/8 CUP ROSEMARY

ESSENTIAL OILS
30 DROPS COCONUT
20 DROPS SAGE
20 DROPS EUCALYPTUS
20 DROPS DRAGON'S BLOOD
30 DROPS VANILLA
30 DROPS YLANG YLANG

DRAGON'S BLOOD PROTECTION CANDLE

HERBAL INGREDIENTS
1/4 CUP RUE
1/8 CUP DRAGON'S BLOOD PWDR.

ESSENTIAL OILS
60 DROPS DRAGON'S BLOOD
30 DROPS SAGE
30 DROPS ROSEMARY
30 DROPS ROSE

HIGH JOHN THE CONQUEROR POWER CANDLE

HERBAL INGREDIENTS
1/2 CUP HIGH JOHN
   THE CONQUEROR ROOT
1/8 CUP LILAC FLOWERS
1/8 CUP ROSES
1/8 CUP LAVENDER FLOWERS

ESSENTIAL OILS
60 DROPS HIGH JOHN
THE CONQUEROR ROOT OIL
40 DROPS LAVENDER
25 DROPS ROSE
25 DROPS YLANG YLANG

COME TO ME CANDLE

HERBAL INGREDIENTS
1/4 CUP CINNAMON POWDER
1/8 CUP ROSES
2 TABLESPOONS PWDRD. PALO VEN A MI
2 TBLSP. PWDRD. PALO AMANSA GUANO
2 TBLSP. POWDERED PALO PARA MI

ESSENTIAL OILS
40 DROPS CINNAMON
30 DROPS ROSE
30 DROPS PATCHOULI
30 DROPS VIOLET
20 DROPS PEPPERMINT

PROSPERITY CANDLE

HERBAL INGREDIENTS
1/8 CUP MINT LEAVES
1/8 CUP VIOLET FLOWERS
1 TABLESPOON NUTMEG POWDER
1/4 CUP ABRE CAMINO HERB

ESSENTIAL OILS
30 DROPS MINT
30 DROPS PEPPERMINT
30 DROPS CARNATION
30 DROPS COCONUT
30 DROPS VANILLA

FAST MONEY DRAWING CANDLE

HERBAL INGREDIENTS
1/4 CUP PATCHOULY ROOT PWDR.
1 TABLESPOON NUTMEG PWDR.
1/8 CUP ROSEMARY LEAVES
1/8 CUP HONEYSUCKLE FLOWERS
1/8 CUP LILAC FLOWERS

ESSENTIAL OILS
30 DROPS HIGH JOHN
THE CONQUEROR OIL
20 DROPS ROSEMARY
30 DROPS ROSE
30 DROPS PEPPERMINT
20 DROPS AMBERGRIS
20 DROPS ORCHID

LUCKY BUSINESS PROSPERITY CANDLE

HERBAL INGREDIENTS
1/8 CUP VIOLETS
1/8 CUP HEATHER FLOWERS
1/2 CUP CINNAMON STICKS
1 TABLESPOON BEE'S HONEY
1/8 CUP ABRE CAMINO HERB

ESSENTIAL OILS
40 DROPS CINNAMON
40 DROPS VANILLA
30 DROPS HISBISCUS
20 DROPS VIOLET
20 DROPS HYSSOP

GET OUT OF JAIL CANDLE

HERBAL INGREDIENTS
2 TBLSP. DEERHORN PWDR.
1 TBLSP. PALO COCUYO
1 TBLSP. PWDED. PALO AMARGO
1 TBLSP. PWDRD. PALO CAMBIA VOZ
1/8 CUP ANISE HERB

ESSENTIAL OILS
50 DROPS MANDRAKE
30 DROPS DRAGON'S BLOOD
40 DROPS ANGELICA
30 DROPS ANISE

SEVEN AFRICAN POWERS CANDLE

HERBAL INGREDIENTS
1/8 CUP ALLSPICE
1/8 CUP MINT LEAVES
1/8 CUP ROSES
1 TBLSP. CINNAMON PWDR.
1/8 CUP ABRE CAMINO HERB
1/8 CUP MARIGOLD FLOWERS
1 TBLSP. PWDRD. PALO VENCE BATALLA

ESSENTIAL OILS
30 DROPS GERANIUM
20 DROPS HONEY
20 DROPS AMBERGRIS
30 DROPS JASMIN
20 DROPS FRANKINCENSE
20 DROPS COCONUT
10 DROPS MYRRH

PALO MAYOMBE DESTRUCTION CANDLE

HERBAL INGREDIENTS
1/8 CUP BLACK PEPPER
1 TBLSP. BLACK SALT
2 TBLSP. PWDRD. PALO MUERTO
2 TBLSP. PWDRD. CAMBIA RUMBA
2 TBLSP. PWDRD. PALO TORCIDO
1 TBLSP. CEMETERY DIRT
1/2 TSP. HUMAN BONE POWDER
1/2 TSP. PWDRD. BAT

ESSENTIAL OILS
1 TBLSP. USED CAR MOTOR
50 DROPS BLACK PEPPER

HOT FOOT CANDLE

HERBAL INGREDIENTS
1/8 CUP RED CHILE PEPPER PWDR.
1 TBLSP. BLACK PEPPER PWDR.
1 TBLSP. PWDRD. PALO VENCE BATALLA
1 TBLSP. PICA PICA PWDR.
1 TBLSP. BLACK SALT

ESSENTIAL OILS
50 DROPS BLACK PEPPER
50 DROPS HIGH JOHN
THE CONQUEROR OIL

CONFLICT CANDLE

INGREDIENTS
2 TBLSP. PWDRD. PALO CAMBIA RUMBA
1 TBLSP. PWDR. PALO BOMBA
1 TBLSP. PWDRD. PALO ESPUELDE GALLO
2 TBLSP. PWDRD. BAT
1 TBLSP. BLACK CAT FUR
1 TBLSP. BLACK DOG FUR

ESSENTIAL OILS
50 DROPS BLACK PEPPER
50 DROPS HIGH JOHN
THE CONQUEROR OIL
50 DROPS HEMLOCK

12

INCENSE

Incense is used by practioners of magic to enhace spells and communication with the spirits and gods. The following incenses are all made from natural ingredients. By burning natural ingredients, you are releasing the magical qualities of the herbs into the universe thus increasing the success rate of a magical spell or ritual. Because some of the following incenses are quite strong in fragrance, they should be burned in a well ventilated area.

THE FOLLOWING IS THE GENERAL FORMULA FOR MAKING POWDERED INCENSE

• Mix all of the ingredients together.
• Place the mixture into a glass storage jar until ready to use.
• When ready to use, place a small amount on a
hot charcoal block.

7 AFRICAN POWERS INCENSE
4 TBLSP. FRANKINCENSE
3 TBLSP. MYRRH
2 TBLSP. CINNAMON PWDR.
1 TBLSP. SAGE PWDR.
1 TBLSP. SANDALWOOD PWDR.
1/2 TBLSP. DRAGON'S BLOOD PWDR.

ELEGGUA PROSPERITY INCENSE
3 TBLSP. NUTMEG PWDR.
2 TBLSP. CINNAMON PWDR.
1 TBLSP. SANDALWOOD PWDR.
1/2 TBLSP. ABRE CAMINO PWDR.
7 DROPS COCONUT OIL
3 DROPS BLUE BONNET OIL

CHANGO DOMINATION INCENSE
3 TBLSP. CLOVE PWDR.
1 TBLSP. DRAGON'S BLOOD PWDR.
1/2 TBLSP. DAMÍANA HERB
1 TBLSP. FRANKINCENSE
7 DROPS EVERGREEN OIL

YEMAYA PEACE INCENSE
1 TBLSP. BAY LEAVES
2 TBLSP. MYRRH
2 TBLSP. COPAL
1 TBLSP. DRIED SEAWEED
1 TBLSP. LILACS
7 DROPS ASTER OIL

OCHUN LOVE INCENSE
3 TBLSP. CINNAMON PWDR.
2 TBLSP. ALLSPICE PWDR.
1 TBLSP. CEDARWOOD PWDR.
1 TBLSP. ROSES
1 TBLSP. CLOVE PWDR.
1 TBLSP. PWDRD.
   PALO AMANSA GUAPO

OBATALA REVERSE INCENSE
3 TBLSP. COPAL
2 TBLSP. JUNIPER BERRIES
1 TBLSP. FRANKINCENSE
1 TBLSP. THYME PWDR.
1/2 TBLSP. KOSHER ROCK SALT
7 DROPS EUCALYPTUS OIL

BABALU-AYE
HEALING INCENSE
3 TBLSP. ROSEMARY
1 TBLSP. FRANKINCENSE
1 TBLSP. SANDALWOOD
1 TBLSP. PATCHOULY

OCHOSI COURT VICTORY
INCENSE
2 TBLSP. DEERHORN PWDR.
1 TBLSP. DRAGON'S BLOOD
2 TBLSP. FRANKINCENSE
1 TBLSP. SAGE
1/2 TBLSP. PWDRD.
   PALO ESPANTA POLICIA

AQUARIUS INCENSE
3 TBLSP. SANDALWOOD
1 TBLSP. CINNAMON
1 TBLSP. COPAL
1 TBLSP. FRANKINCENSE
2 TBLSP. LILAC FLOWERS
7 DROPS AQUARIOUS OIL

LIBRA INCENSE
3 TBLSP. CEDARWOOD
1 TBLSP. PINE RESIN
1 TBLSP. CLOVE
1 TBLSP. COPAL
7 DROPS LIBRA OIL

CANCER INCENSE
3 TBLSP. PINE RESIN
1 TBLSP. CEDAR
1 TBLSP. THYME
1 TBLSP. JUNIPER
7 DROPS CANCER OIL

LEO INCENSE
3 TBLSP. CINNAMON PWDR.
2 TBLSP. DRAGON'S BLOOD PWDR.
2 TBLSP. ALLSPICE
1/2 TBLSP. PWDRD. PALO
   VENCE BATALLA
7 DROPS LEO OIL

VIRGO INCENSE
3 TBLSP. ALLSPICE
3 TBLSP. PINE
1 TBLSP. SAGE
3TBLSP. COPAL
7 DROPS VIRGO OIL

ARIES INCENSE
3 TBLSP. SAGE
3 TBLSP. CINNAMON
3 TBLSP. ROSEMARY
3 TBLSP. FRANKINCENSE
7 DROPS ARIES OIL

GEMINI INCENSE
3 TBLSP. THYME
3 TBLSP. JUNIPER
2 TBLSP. MINT
1 TBLSP. MYRRH
7 DROPS GEMINI OIL

CAPRICORN INCENSE
3 TBLSP. CINNAMON
2 TBLSP. ALLSPICE
1 TBLSP. SANDALWOOD
7 DROPS CAPRICORN OIL

PISCES INCENSE
3 TBLSP. CEDARWOOD
1 TBLSP. FRANKINCENSE
1 TBLSP. COPAL
7 DROPS PISCES OIL

SAGITTARIUS INCENSE
3 TBLSP. DRAGON'S BLOOD PWDR
2 TBLSP. ROSEMARY
2 TBLSP. SANDALWOOD
7 DROPS SAGITTARIUS OIL

TAURUS INCENSE
3 TBLSP. COPAL
3 TBLSP. SANDALWOOD PWDR.
2 TBLSP. CINNAMON PWDR.
7 DROPS TAURUS OIL

SCORPIO INCENSE
3 TBLSP. JUNIPER
1 TBLSP. DRAGON'S BLOOD PWDR.
3 TBLSP. CINNAMON PWDR.
1 TBLSP. ALLSPICE
7 DROPS SCORPIO OIL

PURIFICATION INCENSE
3 TBLSP. SAGE
1 TBLSP. FRANKINCENSE
1 TBLSP. MYRRH
1 TBLSP. ROSEMARY
1 TBLSP. KOSHER ROCK SALT

FAST LUCK / MONEY DRAWING INCENSE
3 TBLSP. CINNAMON
1 TBLSP. CEDAR
1 TBLSP. ABRE CAMINO HERB
1 TBLSP. HIGH JOHN THE
   CONQUEROR ROOT POWDER

FAST LOVE INCENSE
3 TBLSP. CINNAMON
2 TBLSP. ROSES
5 DROPS LILAC OIL
5 DROPS HONEY OIL

UNCROSSING INCENSE
2 TBLSP. DRAGON'S BLOOD
1 TBLSP. PWDRD. EGGSHELL
1 TBLSP. KOSHER ROCK SALT
9 DROPS SAGE OIL

DOMINATION INCENSE
4 TBLSP. DRAGON'S BLOOD PWDR.
2 TBLSP. BAY
1 TBLSP. ALLSPICE
7 DROPS CIVIT OIL

REVERSE EVIL EYE INCENSE
3 TBLSP. RUE
3 TBLSP. DRAGON'S BLOOD PWDR.
1 TBLSP. COFFEE GROUNDS
7 DROPS SANDALWOOD OIL

JINX REMOVAL INCENSE
3 TBLSP. CLOVE
1 TBLSP. GARLIC
1 TBLSP. COPAL
7 DROPS DRAGON'S BLOOD OIL

LUCKY GAMBLER INCENSE
3 TBLSP. ALLSPICE
1 TBLSP. PINE RESIN
7 DROPS HEATHER OIL
7 DROPS PATCHOULY OIL

DESTROY YOUR ENEMIES INCENSE
1 TBLSP. PWDRD. HUMAN BONE
1/2 TBLSP. PWDRD. PALO MUERTO
1 /2 TBLSP. PWDRD PALO
   VENCEBATALLA
2 TBLSP. DRAGON'S BLOOD PWDR.
9 DROPS BLACK PEPPER OIL
9 DROPS REVERSE OIL

PEACEFUL HOME INCENSE
3 TBLSP. CINNAMON
2 TBLSP. CEDARWOOD
1 TBLSP. PINE RESIN
1 TBLSP. LILAC FLOWERS

GUARDIAN ANAGEL INCENSE
3 TBLSP. COPAL
1 TBLSP. ROSES
1 TBLSP. HEATHER
7 DROPS CARNATION OIL
3 DROPS COCONUT OIL

SPIRITUAL COMMUNICATION INCENSE
3 TBLSP. SANDALWOOD
2 TBLSP. FRANKINCENSE
7 DROPS WISTERIA OIL

FAST JOB INCENSE
3 TBLSP. NUTMEG
1/2 TBLSP. ABRE CAMINO HERB
1 TBLSP. SANDALWOOD POWDER
3 DROPS BLUE BONNET OIL
3 DROPS ORRIS OIL
7 DROPS COCONUT OIL

SPELL BREAKER INCENSE
3 TBLSP. DRAGONS BLOOD
1 TBLSP. RUE
1 TBLSP. ROSEMARY
3 DROPS SAGE OIL

COURT VICTORY INCENSE
3 TBLSP. SAGE
1/2 TBLSP. DEERHORN PWDR.
1/2 TBLSP. PWDRD. PALO CAMBIA VOZ
7 DROPS ANGELICA OIL

SEPARATION INCENSE
1 TBLSP. BLACK PEPPER
1/2 TTBLSP. PWDRD. PALO CAMBIA RUMBA
7 DROPS BALSAMO INTRAQUILO OIL
7 DROPS HEMLOCK OIL

PALO MAYOMBE DESTRUCTION INCENSE
1 TBLSP. POWDERED HUMAN BONE
1 TBLSP. SNAKE POWDER
1/2 TBLSP. POWDERED PALO MUERTO
1 TBLSP. DRAGON'S BLOOD POWDER
7 DROPS BLACK PEPPER OIL

PALO MAYOMBE DIVINE JUSTICE INCENSE
1 TBLSP. POWDERED HUMAN BONE
1 TBLSP. DRAGON'S BLOOD POWDER
1/2 TBLSP. DEERHORN POWDER
1/2 TBLSP. PWDRD. PALO JUSTICIA
7 DROPS SANDALWOOD OIL

PALO MAYOMBE LOVE INCENSE
1 PWDRD. HUMAN BONE
1 TBLSP. HUMMINGBIRD POWDER
1 TBLSP. PWDRD. PALO DULCE
7 DROPS ROSE OIL
7 DROPS VIOLET OIL

PALO MAYOMBE SPIRIT INCENSE
1 TBLSP. PWDRD. HUMAN BONE
1 TBLSP. PWDRD. QUARTZ CRYSTAL
1/2 TBLSP. PWDRD. PALO RAMON
7 DROPS SPEARMINT OIL

COME TO ME INCENSE
1 TBLSP. PWDRD. PALO VEN A MI
1 TBLSP. PWDRD. PALO AMANSA GUAPO
1 TBLSP. HUMMINGBIRD POWDER
3 TBLSP. CINNAMON POWDER
7 DROPS ROSE OIL
7 DROPS PATCHOULY OIL

HIGH JOHN THE CONQUEROR INCENSE
3 TBLSP. HIGH JOHN THE CONQUEROR ROOT PWDR.
3 TBLSP. CINNAMON PWDR.
2 TBLSP. DRAGON'S BLOOD PWDR.
1 TBLSP. SANDALWOOD PWDR.
7 DROPS HIGH JOHN THE CONQUEROR OIL

FERTILITY INCENSE
3 TBLSP. ROSEMARY
1 TBLSP. ROSES
1 TBLSP. THYME
7 DROPS COCONUT OIL
7 DROPS WATERMELON OIL
3 DROPS CHRYSANTHEMUM OIL

HEXING INCENSE
1 TBLSP. BAT POWDER
1 TBLSP. PWDRD. BLACK CAT BONE
1 TBLSP. PWDRD. PALO TORCIDO
7 DROPS BLACK PEPPER OIL

SEVEN HOLY ANGELS INCENSE
3 TBLSP. CINNAMON POWDER
1 TBLSP. ALLSPICE
1 TBLSP. SANDALWOOD
1 TBLSP. PINE RESIN
3 DROPS COCONUT OIL
7 DROPS 7 AFRICAN POWERS OIL
3 DROPS MUSK OIL
3 DROPS ROSE OIL

BETTER BUSINESS INCENSE
3 TBLSP. CINNAMON POWER
1 TBLSP. LILAC FLOWERS
1 TBLSP. CEDAR
1 TBLSP. SANDALWOOD
7 DROPS MONEY DRAWING OIL
3 DROPS VIOLET OIL
3 DROPS VANILLA OIL

LUCKY LOTTO INCENSE
3 TBLSP. PINE NEEDLES
1 TBLSP. NUTMEG PWDR.
2 TBLSP. CINNAMON PWDR.
1 TBLSP. CEDARWOOD PWDR.
2 TBLSP. HIGH JOHN THE CONQUEROR ROOT PWDR.
3 DROPS BERGAMOT OIL
3 DROPS CLOVER OIL
3 DROPS HEATHER OIL

13

FLOOR WASH

I can remember as a small child waking up to the sound of splashing water and then intense scrubbing. This sound so familar was my grandmother washing the entrance to our home with a particular scented water mixture. The herbal / water mixture was called floor wash which she believed would take away the evil eye and protect our home. The use of floor washes by Latin American Spiritualists is quite common. Spiritualists believe that by washing an area with a specially prepared herbal mixture they are bringing out the magical properties of the herbs which make up the floor wash. Floor washes can be used for such things as to attract love, luck, money and for protection. Many spiritualists believe that floor washes will enhance a magical spell and bring about better results.The following are some of the most popular and traditional floor washes used by Latin American spiritualists.

GENERAL FORMULA FOR
MAKING FLOOR WASH

• *Boil all of the ingredients for 20 minutes in 1 quart of water.*
• *Allow the liquid mixture to cool.*
• *Add 1 cup of ammonia to the liquid mixture.*
• *Add 1/2 cup of Spiritual Water.*
• *Pour the liquid mixture into a plastic storage bottle until ready to use.*
• *Allow the liquid mixture to remain in bottle for 7 days before using.*

TO USE
• *Add 2 cups of Floor Wash to 1 gallon of water.*
• *Wash the inside and outside of your home or business.*

SIMPLE FLOOR WASH
This floor wash is used for general spiritual house cleansings.
1 CUP OF RUE
1/2 LIME JUICE
2 CUPS OF KOSHER ROCK SALT
HOLY WATER (SPIRITUAL WATER)
1 CUP KOLONIA 1800 (SPIRITUAL WATER)

BITTER HERB FLOOR WASH
A good general floor wash used to banish negativity and witchcraft.
1 CUP SAGE
1 CUP ROSEMARY
1 CUP LIME JUICE
1 CUP RUE
1 CUP KOSHER ROCK SALT
FLORIDA WATER (SPIRITUAL WATER)

SWEET HERB FLOOR WASH
A good general floor wash to bring prosperity, luck, love and protection.
1 CUP ROSES
1 CUP LILACS
1 CUP MINT
1 CUP CINNAMON STICKS
FLORIDA WATER (SPIRITUAL WATER)

OLODUMARE'S PURIFICATION FLOOR WASH
This floor wash is used to purify a ritual area.
1 CUP OF SUN FLOWER PETALS
1 CUP PASSION FLOWERS
1 CUP WHITE CARNATIONS
1 CUP KOSHER ROCK SALT
ROSE WATER (SPIRITUAL WATER)

SEVEN AFRICAN POWERS FLOOR WASH
This floor wash brings success, protection, luck, love and money.
1 CUP ABRE CAMINO HERB
1 CUP GARDENIA FLOWERS
1 CUP VIOLETS
1 CUP ROSEMARY
1 CUP PEPPERMINT
KOLONIA 1800 (SPIRITUAL WATER)

ELEGGUA PROSPERITY FLOOR WASH
This floor wash brings prosperity and wealth.
1 CUP GUAYABA LEAVES
1 CUP ABRE CAMINO HERB
1 CUP CINNAMON STICKS
VIOLET WATER (SPIRITUAL WATER)

YEMAYA'S PEACE FLOOR WASH
This floor wash will bring peace and protection to a troubled home.
1 CUP CHRYSANTHEMUM FLOWERS
1 CUP PALO DULCE
1 CUP SEA SALT
1 TABLESPOON ANIL
FLORIDA WATER (SPIRITUAL WATER)

OCHUN'S LOVE FLOOR WASH
This floor wash brings love to a home or attraction to an individual.
1 CUP YELLOW ROSES
2 CUPS CINNAMON STICKS
2 CUP PATCHOULY ROOTS
ROSE WATER (SPIRITUAL WATER)
ORANGE WATER (SPIRITUAL WATER)

CHANGO'S PROTECTION FLOOR WASH

This floor wash protects against attacks from enemies and witchcraft.
1 CUP PALO VENCE BATALLA
1 CUP HEATHER FLOWERS
1 CUP LAVENDER FLOWERS
1 CUP PEPPERMINT
SIETE MACHOS COLOGNE
(SPIRITUAL WATER)

SAN LAZARO'S HEALING FLOOR WASH

This floor wash is used to remove the spirit of sickness.
1 CUP SHREDDED COCONUT
1 CUP EUCALYPTUS LEAVES
1 CUP RUE
1 CUP ROSEMARY
FLORIDA WATER *(SPIRITUAL WATER)*

REVERSE EVIL FLOOR WASH

This floor wash is used to reverse the evil eye or witchcraft.
1 CUP PALO CABALLERO
1 CUP PALO AMARGO
1 CUP RUE
1 CUP ROSEMARY
1 CUP KOSHER ROCK SALT
FLORIDA WATER (SPIRITUAL WATER)

MONEY DRAWING FLOOR WASH

This floor wash brings fast money and prosperity.
1 CUP ROMAINE LETTUCE
1 CUP ROSE OF JERICO
1 CUP HIGH JOHN CONQUEROR ROOT
1 CUP CINNAMON STICKS
VIOLET WATER (SPIRITUAL WATER)

SAN MARTIN CABALLERO BUSINESS FLOOR WASH

This foor wash is used to draw in customers and money to a business.
1 CUP BROWN MUSTARD SEEDS
1 CUP ANISE
1 CUP PALO VEN A MI
1 CUP CINNAMON SHCKS
LAVANDA WATER (SPIRITUAL WATER)

HIGH JOHN THE CONQUEROR FLOOR WASH

This floor wash is used for protection, success and prosperity.
2 CUPS HIGH JOHN CONQUEROR ROOT
1 CUP FIVE FINGER GRASS
1 CUP LEMON GRASS
SIETE MACHOS COLOGNE
(SPIRITUAL WATER)

FAST LUCK FLOOR WASH

This floor wash brings prosperity and luck to an individual.
1 CUP CLOVES
1 CUP ROSEMARY
1 CUP LILAC FLOWERS
1 CUP MARIGOLD FLOWERS
ORANGE WATER *(SPIRITUAL WATER)*

PROSPERITY FLOOR WASH

This floor wash opens the doors to success and prosperity.
1 CUP ABRE CAMINO HERB
1 CUP CINNAMON STICKS
1 CUP BAY LEAVES
1 CUP GUAYABA LEAVES
KOLONIA 1800 *(SPIRITUAL WATER)*

ESPANTA POLICIA FLOOR WASH

This floor wash keeps the law away from a business or home.
1 CUP PALO ESPANTA POLICIA
1 CUP LICORICE STICKS HERB
1 CUP ANISE
1 TBLSP. DEERHORN POWDER
FLORIDA WATER *(SPIRITUAL WATER)*

ESPANTA MUERTO FLOOR WASH

This floor wash is used to get rid of an evil spirit.
2 CUPS PALO ESPANTA MUERTO
1 CUP OF LIME JUICE
1 CUP KOSHER ROCK SALT
1 CUP RUE
FLORIDA WATER *(SPIRITUAL WATER)*

COME TO ME FLOOR WASH

This floor wash is used to attract an
individual to you.
1 CUP ABRE CAMINO HERB
1 CUP PALO VEN A MI
1 CUP CINNAMON STICKS
1 CUP PALO AMANSA GUAPO
SECRETS OF CLEOPATRA PERFUME
(SPIRITUAL WATER)

PURIFICATION FLOOR WASH

This floor wash is used to banish
negativity and evil spirits.
1 CUP PINE NEEDLES
1/2 CUP CLOVES
1/2 CUP CINNAMON STICKS
1 CUP SAGE
1 TBLSP. PWDRD. QUARTZ CRYSTALS
VIOLET WATER *(SPIRITUAL WATER)*

FAST MONEY FLOOR WASH

This floor wash is used to give
gamblers fast luck.
1 CUP PINE NEEDLES
1 CUP PATCHOULY ROOT
1 CUP PEPPERMINT LEAVES
1 CUP BOTON DE ORO HERB
1 CUP BASIL
7 AFRICAN POWERS PERFUME WATER
(SPIRITUAL WATER)

COME TO ME FLOOR WASH

This floor wash is used to attract an
individual to you.
1 CUP ABRE CAMINO HERB
1 CUP PALO VEN A MI
1 CUP CINNAMON STICKS
1 CUP PALO AMANSA GUAPO
SECRETS OF CLEOPATRA PERFUME
(SPIRITUAL WATER)

PURIFICATION FLOOR WASH

This floor wash is used to banish
negativity and evil spirits.
1 CUP PINE NEEDLES
1/2 CUP CLOVES
1/2 CUP CINNAMON SHCKS
1 CUP SAGE
1 TBLSP. PWDRD. QUARTZ CRYSTALS
VIOLET WATER *(SPIRITUAL WATER)*

FAST MONEY FLOOR WASH

This floor wash is used to give
gamblers fast luck.
1 CUP PINE NEEDLES
1 CUP PATCHOULY ROOT
1 CUP PEPPERMINT LEAVES
1 CUP BOTON DE ORO HERB
1 CUP BASIL
7 AFRICAN POWERS PERFUME WATER
(SPIRITUAL WATER)

PEACEFUL HOME FLOOR WASH

This floor wash is used to bring peace
and tranquility to a home.
1 CUP GARDENIA FLOWERS
1 CUP VIOLET FLOWERS
1 CUP LILAC FLOWERS
1 CUP SEA SALT
FLORIDA WATER *(SPIRITUAL WATER)*

COURT VICTORY FLOOR WASH

This floor wash is used to win
a court battle.
1 CUP TOBACCO LEAVES
I CUP SAGE
1 CUP SASSAFRAS
1 CUP ANISE
1 TBLSP. DEERHORN POWDER
SIETE MACHOS COLOGNE
(SPIRITUAL WATER)

FAST JOB FLOOR WASH

This floor wash opens the doors to
job and career opportunities.
1 CUP NUTMEG
1 CUP ABRE CAMINO HERB
1 CUP AMANSA GUAPO HERB
1 CUP ROSE PETALS
ORANGE WATER *(SPIRITUAL WATER)*

DRAGON'S BLOOD FLOOR WASH

This floor wash is used to banish evil
spirits and anger directed at you
1 CUP DRAGON'S BLOOD POWDER
1 CUP HIGH JOHN THE
CONQUEROR ROOT
1 CUP QUINTA MALDICION HERB
1 CUP KOSHER ROCK SALT
1 CUP ESPANTA MUERTO HERB
FLORIDA WATER *(SPIRITUAL WATER)*

SPIRITUAL GUIDE FLOOR WASH

This floor wash is used to bring your guardian angel closer to you.
1 CUP GERANIUM FLOWERS (WHITE)
1 CUP VIOLET FLOWERS
1 CUP CARNATION FLOWERS
1 CUP CAMPANA BLANCA FLOWERS
1 CUP CINNAMON STICKS
FLORIDA WATER *(SPIRITUAL WATER)*
HOLY WATER *(SPIRITUAL WATER)*

MEDITATION FLOOR WASH

This floor wash is used to banish negativity from a room or home.
1 CUP GARDENIA FLOWERS
1 CUP SANDALWOOD
1 CUP HEATHER FLOWERS
1/4 CUP SAGE
KOLONIA 1800 *(SPIRITUAL WATER)*

OVERCOME YOUR ENEMIES FLOOR WASH

This floor wash is used to conquer your enemies
1 TBLSP. PWDRD. PALO VENCE BATALLA
1 TBLSP. PWDRD. PALO CABALLERO
1 TBLSP. PWDRD. PALO NEGRO
1 CUP RUE
1 CUP ROSEMARY
KOLONIA 1800 *(SPIRITUAL WATER)*
SIETE MACHOS COLOGNE
  (SPIRITUAL WATER)

CASA DE SANTO FLOOR WASH

This floor wash is used to bring prosperity and protection.
1 CUP BOTON DE ORO
1 CUP MINT
1 CUP CINNAMON STICKS
1 CUP PARAISO HERB
1 CUP RUE
1 CUP ABRE CAMINO HERB
KOLONIA 1800 *(SPIRITUAL WATER)*
FLORIDA WATER *(SPIRITUAL WATER)*
ORANGE WATER *(SPIRITUAL WATER)*
URINE *(USE AS A SPIRITUAL WATER)*

*THE URINE SHOULD BE FROM THE PRIMARY SANTERO.

CASA DE LOS ESPIRITUS FLOOR WASH

This floor wash is used to bring blessings and protection from the spirits.
1 CUP GUAYABA LEAVES
1 TBLSP. PWDRD.PALO RAMON
1 TBLSP. PWDRD. PALO GUASIMO
1 TBLSP. PALO MALAMBO
1 TBLSP. PWDRD. PALO CLAVO
1 CUP RUE
1 CUP ROSEMARY
1 TBLSP. PWDRD. BLACK DOG BONES
  (LEGS AND HEAD)
HOLY WATER *(SPIRITUAL WATER)*
KOLONIA 1800 *(SPIRITUAL WATER)*
URINE *(USE A SPIRITUAL WATER)*

*THE URINE SHOULD BE FROM THE PRIMARY PALERO.

PUERTO RICAN SPIRITUALISTS FLOOR WASH

This floor wash is used to bring prosperity, blessings and protection.
1 CUP RED ROSES
1 CUP WHITE ROSES
1 CUP MINT
1 CUP PEPPERMINT
1 CUP RUE
1 CUP GUAYABA LEAVES
1 TBLSP. PWDRD. PALO ABRE CAMINO
HOLY WATER *(SPIRITUAL WATER)*
FLORIDA WATER *(SPIRITUAL WATER)*

MONTENEGRO
SPECIAL FLOOR WASH

This is my own secret recipe for one of my own floor wash that I have used with much success. The floor wash is used to get rid of witchcraft, negative vibrations and to bring prosperity to a business or home. The general formula does not apply to this recipe.

INGREDIENTS

1. *Twenty-One fresh herbs sacred to the Orishas*
2. *River Water*
3. *May Rain Water*
4. *Holy Water*
5. *Sea Water*
6. *Coconut Water*
7. *1 tblsp. Cascarilla (Eggshell powder)*
8. *Kolonia 1800 (Spiritual water)*
9. *Florida Water (Spiritual water)*
10. *Orange Water (Spiritual water)*
11. *Siete Machos Cologne (Spiritual water)*

PREPARATION

1. *Pour all of the waters into a large metal basin.*
2. *Place all of the fresh herbs and cascarilla in the basin .*
3. *Using your hands, shred the herbs and mix into the waters.*
4. *Place a white candle next to the basin and allow to remain for 24 hours.*
5. *The floor wash is ready to use after 24 hours.*

14

BATH CRYSTALS

Bath Crystals can be created and used in magical bath rituals. Bath crystals can be made by using a number of items and spiritual oils. The following formulas are the most popular used by spirituialists.

THE GENERAL FORMULA FOR
MAKING BATH CRYSTALS

- *Place 3 1/2 cups Kosher Rock Salt in a mixing bowl.*
- *Add 2 cups Baking Soda to the mixing bowl.*
- *Add 1/2 cup Sea Salt to the mixing bowl.*
- *Add all of the ingredients to the mixing bowl.*
- *If desired, you may color the crystals with food coloring.*
- *Mix and store in a storage jar until ready to use.*

BITTER BATH CRYSTALS
30 DROPS RUE OIL
30 DROPS SAGE OIL
30 DROPS DRAGON'S BLOOD OIL
30 DROPS ROSEMARY OIL

SWEET BATH CRYSTALS
30 DROPS ROSE OIL
30 DROPS MINT OIL
30 DROPS PEPPERMINT OIL
30 DROPS LILAC OIL

COCONUT BATH CRYSTALS
120 DROPS COCONUT OIL

LILAC BATH CRYSTALS
120 DROPS LILAC OIL

LAVENDER BATH CRYSTALS
120 DROPS LAVENDER OIL

DRAGON'S BLOOD BATH CRYSTALS
120 DROPS OF DRAGON'S BLOOD OIL

SEVEN AFRICAN POWERS
30 DROPS ALLSPICE OIL
30 DROPS AMBROSIA OIL
30 DROPS COCONUT OIL
30 DROPS PEPPERMINT OIL

ELEGGUA SUCCESS
30 DROPS COCONUT OIL
30 DROPS NUTMEG OIL
30 DROPS HEATHER OIL
30 DROPS MINT OIL

ELEGGUA MONEY DRAWING
30 DROPS SPEARMINT OIL
30 DROPS PEPPERMINT OIL
30 DROPS COCONUT OIL
15 DROPS SASSAFRAS OIL
15 DROPS ANISE OIL

ORISHA OBATALA PURIFICATION
30 DROPS ASTER OIL
30 DROPS COCONUT OIL
15 DROPS SAGE OIL
15 DROPS EUCALYPTUS OIL
30 DROPS VIOLET OIL

YEMAYA PEACE DRAWING
30 DROPS CHRYSANTHEUM OIL
30 DROPS LILAC OIL
30 DROPS HYACINTH OIL
30 DROPS WATERMELON OIL

OCHUN'S LOVE
30 DROPS CINNAMON OIL
30 DROPS LILAC OIL
30 DROPS HONEY OIL
30 DROPS AMBERGRIS OIL

YEMAYA OLOCUN STABILITY
30 DROPS ASTER OIL
40 DROPS COCONUT OIL
50 DROPS WATERMELON OIL

CHANGO'S VICTORY
30 DROPS SANDALWOOD OIL
30 DROPS VERTIVERT OIL
30 DROPS APPLE OIL
30 DROPS HISHISCUS OIL

OCHOSI'S COURT VICTORY
1 TBLSPN. DEERHORN POWDER
30 DROPS ALMOND OIL
30 DROPS ANISE OIL
30 DROPS PINE OIL
30 DROPS ANGELICA OIL

SAN LAZARO HEALING
30 DROPS COCONUT OIL
20 DROPS SAGE OIL
20 DROPS MYRRH OIL
30 DROPS CEDAR OIL
20 DROPS COCONUT OIL

ORUNLA'S PROPHECY
30 DROPS ACACIA OIL
30 DROPS COCONUT OIL
30 DROPS PEPPERMINT OIL
30 DROPS FRANKINCENSE OIL

AQUARIUS
30 DROPS PATCHOULY OIL
30 DROPS LAVENDER OIL
30 DROPS PEPPERMINT OIL
30 DROPS VIOLET OIL

LIBRA
30 DROPS ORCHID OIL
30 DROPS VANILLA OIL
30 DROPS ROSE OIL
30 DROPS PLUMERIA OIL

ARIES
30 DROPS CARNATION OIL
30 DROPS JUNIPER OIL
30 DROPS DRAGON'S BLOOD OIL
30 DROPS CINNAMON OIL

CANCER
30 DROPS VIOLET OIL
30 DROPS LILAC OIL
30 DROPS LEMON OIL
30 DROPS AMBERGRIS OIL

GEMINI
30 DROPS LAVENDER OIL
30 DROPS PEPPERMINT OIL
30 DROPS ALMOND OIL
30 DROPS LILY OIL

CAPRICORN
30 DROPS HONEYSUCKLE OIL
30 DROPS PATCHOULY OIL
30 DROPS VERTIVERT OIL
30 DROPS CYPRESS OIL

LEO
30 DROPS ROSEMARY OIL
30 DROPS MUSK OIL
30 DROPS CINNAMON OIL
15 DROPS AMBERGRIS OIL
15 DROPS ACACIA OIL

PISCES
50 DROPS ANISE OIL
30 DROPS JASMINE OIL
30 DROPS HONEYSUCKLE OIL
10 DROPS NUTMEG OIL

SAGITTARIUS
30 DROPS ROSE OIL
30 DROPS GINGER OIL
20 DROPS SAGE OIL
40 DROPS CEDAR OIL

TAURUS
30 DROPS LILAC OIL
30 DROPS VANILLA OIL
30 DROPS VIOLET OIL
30 DROPS ROSE OIL

VIRGO
30 DROPS LILY OIL
30 DROPS HONEYSUCKLE OIL
30 DROPS BERGAMOT OIL
30 DROPS LAVENDER OIL

SCORPIO
30 DROPS AMBERGRIS OIL
15 DROPS MUSK OIL
15 DROPS CLOVE OIL
30 DROPS VIOLET OIL
30 DROPS GARDENIA OIL

COME TO ME
30 DROPS CINNAMON OIL
30 DROPS YLANG YLANG OIL
30 DROPS AMBERGRIS OIL
30 DROPS VANILLA OIL

CONQUERING
30 DROPS ALLSPICE OIL
30 DROPS VANILLA OIL
30 DROPS CINNAMON OIL
30 DROPS DRAGON'S BLOOD OIL

GET RID OF EVIL
30 DROPS DRAGON'S BLOOD OIL
30 DROPS PEPPERMINT OIL
30 DROPS ANGELICA OIL
30 DROPS MISTLETOE OIL

SPELL BREAKING
30 DROPS SANDALWOOD OIL
30 DROPS MYRRH OIL
30 DROPS LILAC OIL
30 DROPS ANISE OIL

STEADY WORK
30 DROPS HEATHER OIL
30 DROPS VIOLET OIL
30 DROPS ROSE OIL
30 DROPS VERTIVERT OIL

HEALING
30 DROPS COCONUT OIL
30 DROPS SANDALWOOD OIL
30 DROPS VIOLET OIL
30 DROPS EUCALYPTUS OIL

LUCKY GAMBLING
30 DROPS CARNATION OIL
30 DROPS PATCHOULY OIL
30 DROPS JASMINE OIL
15 DROPS CINNAMON OIL
15 DROPS ANISE OIL

QUICK MARRIAGE
30 DROPS LAVENDER OIL
30 DROPS VANILLA OIL
30 DROPS AMBERGRIS OIL
25 DROPS CINNAMON OIL
15 DROPS MUSK OIL

PROSPERITY
30 DROPS VIOLET OIL
30 DROPS ROSE OIL
30 DROPS PINE OIL
30 DROPS CINNAMON OIL

BETTER BUSINESS
30 DROPS COCONUT OIL
30 DROPS HYSSOP OIL
30 DROPS VIOLET OIL
30 DROPS HEATHER OIL

DO AS I SAY
30 DROPS VANILLA OIL
30 DROPS ROSEMARY OIL
30 DROPS FRANKINCENSE OIL
30 DROPS AMBERGRIS OIL

BANISHING
30 DROPS MYRRH OIL
30 DROPS FRANKINCENSE OIL
30 DROPS DRAGON'S BLOOD OIL
30 DROPS PEPPERMINT OIL

APHRODISIAC
30 DROPS AMBERGRIS OIL
30 DROPS VANILLA OIL
30 DROPS CINNAMON OIL
15 DROPS MUSK OIL
15 DROPS HISBISCUS OIL

DOMINATION
30 DROPS YLANG YLANG OIL
30 DROPS ALLSPICE OIL
30 DROPS VIOLET OIL
30 DROPS VANILLA OIL

QUEEN CLEOPATRA ATTRACTION
30 DROPS CINNAMON OIL
30 DROPS VIOLET OIL
15 DROPS PEPPERMINT OIL
15 DROPS VANILLA OIL
30 DROPS AMBERGRIS OIL

MONTENEGRO FAST MONEY
30 DROPS NUTMEG OIL
30 DROPS HONEYSUCKLE OIL
30 DROPS CINNAMON OIL
30 DROPS HYSSOP OIL

MONTENEGRO FAST LUCK
30 DROPS PATCHOULY OIL
30 DROPS VERTIVERT OIL
30 DROPS PINE OIL
30 DROPS CINNAMON OIL

BIG MONEY
30 DROPS CARNATION OIL
30 DROPS VANILLA OIL
30 DROPS LILAC OIL
30 DROPS SASSAFRAS OIL

LUCKY LOTTO
30 DROPS ALLSPICE OIL
30 DROPS SAGE OIL
30 DROPS CLOVER OIL
30 DROPS CEDARWOOD OIL

UNCROSSING
30 DROPS COCONUT OIL
30 DROPS LILAC OIL
15 DROPS SAGE OIL
15 DROPS MYRRH OIL
15 DROPS FRANKINCENSE OIL
15 DROPS ROSEMARY OIL

JUST JUDGE
30 DROPS DRAGON'S BLOOD OIL
30 DROPS RUE OIL
30 DROPS MANDRAKE OIL
30 DROPS HYACINTH OIL

LOVE DROPS
30 DROPS CINNAMON OIL
30 DROPS VANILLA OIL
30 DROPS PEPPERMINT OIL
15 DROPS CIVET OIL
15 DROPS PATCHOULY OIL

TRIPLE ACTION REVERSIBLE
30 DROPS PINE OIL
30 DROPS GINGER OIL
30 DROPS DRAGON'S BLOOD OIL
30 DROPS BASIL OIL

ABRE CAMINO
30 DROPS ANISE OIL
30 DROPS NUTMEG OIL
30 DROPS HYSSOP OIL
30 DROPS SASSAFRAS OIL

HOLD MY MAN
30 DROPS YLANG YLANG OIL
30 DROPS ORCHID OIL
30 DROPS TUBEROSE OIL
30 DROPS PLUMERIA OIL

HOLD MY WOMAN
30 DROPS VIOLET OIL
30 DROPS SPEARMINT OIL
30 DROPS ROSE OIL
30 DROPS APPLE OIL

GUARDIAN ANGEL
30 DROPS COCONUT OIL
30 DROPS NUTMEG OIL
30 DROPS CINNAMON OIL
30 DROPS PEPPERMINT OIL

LAW STAY AWAY
30 DROPS SAGE OIL
30 DROPS ANISE OIL
30 DROPS HYSSOP OIL
30 DROPS ANGELICA OIL

HUMMINGBIRD LOVE
30 DROPS HONEYSUCKLE OIL
30 DROPS LILAC OIL
30 DROPS ROSE OIL
30 DROPS PLUMERIA OIL

HIGH JOHN THE CONQUEROR
30 DROPS LAVENDER OIL
30 DROPS DRAGON'S BLOOD OIL
30 DROPS YLANG YLANG OIL
30 DROPS PATCHOULI OIL

7 DAY QUICK UNCROSSING
30 DROPS COCONUT OIL
30 DROPS CLOVE OIL
30 DROPS LAVENDER OIL
30 DROPS DRAGON'S BLOOD OIL

STEADY WORK
30 DROPS LERNONGRASS OIL
30 DROPS HYSSOP OIL
30 DROPS ROSE OIL
30 DROPS SAGE OIL

LUCKY GAMBLER
30 DROPS CINNAMON OIL
30 DROPS ROSE OIL
30 CROPS HONEYSUCKLE OIL
30 DROPS JASMINE OIL

BALSAMO TRANQUILLO
60 DROPS BALSAM OIL
20 DROPS ROSE OIL
20 DROPS VANILLA OIL
20 DROPS LAVENDER OIL

15

HANDMADE SOAPS

Soap should be used on a daily basis to keep your body clean from negative vibrations. Soaps can be made for a variety of special requests and purposes such as in attracting love, luck, prosperity and gambling spells. The following soap formulas are easy to make and use.

GENERAL FORMULA FOR
MAKING LIQUID SOAP

- *Place 2 cups of grated Castile soap into a metal pan.*
- *Place 3 cups water into the pan.*
- *Boil the mixture on a low flame.*
- *When the soap has completely dissolved turn the heat off.*
- *Allow the liquid soap mixture to cool for 7-8 minutes.*
- *Mix all of the ingredients with the soap mixture.*
- *Pour the soap into a glass jar until it is ready to use.*
- *Soap should be placed in the refrigerator to keep its freshness.*

BITTER HERB SOAP
This soap is used to remove negative vibrations from an individual.
1 CUP ESPANTA MUERTO HERB
1/2 CUP RUE
10 DROPS DRAGON'S BLOOD OIL
10 DROPS SAGE OIL

ESPANTA MUERTO SOAP
This soap is used to get rid of an evil spirit from an individual.
1 CUP ESPANTA MUERTO HERB
1/2 CUP RUE
10 DROPS DRAGON'S BLOOD OIL
10 DROPS SAGE OIL

ESPANTA POLICIA SOAP

This soap is used to protect an individual from legal problems.
1 CUP ESPANTA POLICIA HERB
2 TBLSP. DEERHORN POWDER
10 DROPS ANISE OIL
10 DROPS DRAGON'S BLOOD OIL

ABRE CAMINO SOAP

This soap is used to bring success and opportunity to an individual.
1 CUP ABRE CAMINO HERB
1 TBLSP. BOTON DE ORO HERB
1 TBLSP. MINT
10 DROPS PATCHOULY OIL
7 DROPS JASMINE OIL

AMANSA GUAPO SOAP

This soap is used to attract love and prosperity.
1 CUP AMANSA GUAPO HERB
1 TBLSP. POWDERED PALO DULCE
1/4 CUP CINNAMON POWDER
10 DROPS HONEY OIL
7 DROPS AMBERGRIS OIL
7 DROPS PEPPERMINT OIL

RUDA SOAP

This soap is used to remove negativity and the evil eye.
1 CUP RUDA (RUE)
1/2 CUP SAGE
10 DROPS CLOVE OIL
10 DROPS RUE OIL

ALBAHACA SOAP

This soap is used to remove negativity.
1 CUP ALBAHACA
1/2 CUP LILAC FLOWERS
10 DROPS FRANKINCENSE OIL
7 DROPS MYRRH OIL

COCONUT SOAP

This soap is used to dispel negativity and bring clarity of mind.
I TBLSP. CASCARILLA
   (EGGSHELL POWDER)
1 TBLSP. CINNAMON POWDER
1 OUNCE COCONUT OIL
10 DROPS CINNAMON OIL
IO DROPS VANILLA OIL

BRAZILIAN BLACK HERB SOAP

A traditional soap used by Brazilian Spiritualists to banish negativity.
1 TBLSP. SEA SALT
2 TBLSP. SANDALWOOD POWDER
1 TBLSP. BASIL
2 TBLSP. ROSEMARY
1 TBLSP. ALLSPICE
10 DROPS DRAGON'S BLOOD OIL
10 DROPS RUE OIL
10 DROPS SAGE OIL
7 DROPS EUCALYPTUS OIL

ACHE DE SANTO SOAP

This soap is used to banish negativity and bring power to a spiritualist.
2 TBLSP. ACHE DE SANTO HERBS
1 TBLSP. CINNAMON POWDER
1 TBLSP. NUTMEG
1/2 TBLSP. DRAGON'S BLOOD POWDER
1 /2 TBLSP. PALM OIL
10 DROPS COCONUT OIL
10 DROPS EUCALYPTUS OIL

SEVEN AFRICAN POWERS

Use this soap to bring prosperity, luck and protection.
1 TBLSP. CINNAMON POWDER
1 TBLSP. BASIL
1 TBLSP. ALLSPICE
1 TBLSP. ROSES
1 TBLSP. LILACS
10 DROPS COCONUT OIL
7 DROPS LAVENDER
7 DROPS ROSE OIL
5 DROPS YLANG YLANG OIL

ELEGGUA PROSPERITY SOAP

This soap is used to attract opportunity and success.
1 CUP ABRE CAMINO HERB
1 TBLSP. BOTON DE ORO HERB
1 TBLSP. CINNAMON POWDER
1 TBLSP. PWDRD. PALO DE GUAYABA
10 DROPS COCONUT OIL
10 DROPS NUTMEG OIL
7 DROPS VIOLET OIL

OCHUN'S LOVE SOAP

This soap is used to attract love and fortune.
1/2 CUP CINNAMON
1 TBLSP. PWDRD. PALO ABRE CAMINO
1/2 CUP AMANSA GUAPO HERB
15 DROPS HONEY OIL
10 DROPS VANILLA OIL
10 DROPS PATCHOULY OIL
3 DROPS AMBERGRIS OIL

YEMAYA'S PEACE SOAP

This soap is used for protection and to bring peace of mind.
1/4 CUP ANIL
1 TBLSP. SEA SALT
1 CUP DRIED SEAWEED
10 DROPS LILAC OIL
5 DROPS GARDENIA OIL
3 DROPS CHRYSANTHEMUM OIL

YEMAYA'S FERTILITY SOAP

This soap is used to bring fertility.
1/4 CUP ANIL
1 TABLESPOON SEA SALT
1 CUP DRIED SEAWEED
1 TBLSP. PWDRD. PALO DULCE
15 DROPS WATERMELON OIL
5 DROPS LAVENDER OIL

CHANGO'S PROTECTION SOAP

This soap is used to reverse witchcraft and also for protection.
1 CUP PARAISO HERB
1 TBLSP. CLOVE POWDER
1 TBLSP. PEPPERMINT
10 DROPS ROSEMARY OIL
10 DROPS JUNIPER OIL

OBATALA'S PURIFICATION

This soap is used to purify an indiviual before a ritual.
1 TBLSP. SAGE
1 TBLSP. RUE
1 TBLSP. DRAGON'S BLOOD PWDR.
1 TBLSP. CASCARILLA
(EGGSHELL POWDER)
10 DROPS DRAGON'S BLOOD OIL
10 DROPS MYRRH OIL
10 DROPS COCONUT OIL
5 DROPS FRANKINCENSE OIL

SAN LAZARO'S HEALING SOAP

This soap is used to rid the spirit of sickness from an individual.
1 CUP ROSEMARY
1/2 CUP RUE
1 TBLSP. SANDALWOOD PWDR.
1 TBLSP. DRAGON'S BLOOD PWDR.
10 DROPS GARDENIA OIL
10 DROPS SAGE OIL
10 DROPS COCONUT OIL

OCHOSI'S COURT VICTORY

This soap is used to protect an indivdual from prosecution.
1 CUP ANISE HERB
1 TBLSP. MANDRAKE ROOT PWDR.
2 TBLSP. DEERHORN PWDR.
10 DROPS MANDRAKE OIL
10 DROPS DRAGON'S BLOOD OIL

PALO MAYOMBE CLEANSING

This soap is used to remove an evil spirit from an individual.
1 TBLSP. PWDRD. PALO ESPANTA MUERTO
1 TBLSP. PWDRD. PALO VENCE BATALLA
1 TBLSP. PWDRD. PALO CANPECHE
1 TBLSP. QINTA MALDICION HERB
10 DROPS DRAGON'S BLOOD OIL
10 DROPS SAGE OIL
7 DROPS ROSEMARY OIL

PALO MAYOMBE PROSPERITY

This soap is used to bring prosperity and fortune to an individual.
1 CUP ABRE CAMINO HERB
1 TBLSP. DEERHORN POWDER
1 TBLSP. PWDRD. PALO HUESO
1 TBLSP. PWDRD. PALO AMARGO
10 DROPS ANISE OIL
10 DROPS NUTMEG OIL
7 DROPS DRAGON'S BLOOD OIL

PALO MAYOMBE SPIRIT SOAP

This soap is used by a spiritualist to bring them magical powers.
2 TBLSP. PWDRD. PALO GUAMA
1 TBLSP. PWDRD. PALO COCUYO
1 TBLSP. PWDRD. PALO DIABLO
1 TBLSP. HUMAN BONE POWDER
10 DROPS VANILLA OIL
7 DROPS CAMPHOR OIL

MONEY DRAWING SOAP

This soap is bring an individual fast
money and success.
1 CUP MINT
1/4 CUP ABRE CAMINO HERB
1/2 CUP PATCHOULY ROOT POWDER
1 TBLSP. HIGH JOHN THE
CONQUEROR ROOT POWDER
1 TBLSP. CINNAMON POWDER
10 DROPS HIGH JOHN THE
CONQUEROR OIL
10 DROPS 7 AFRICAN POWERS OIL
10 DROPS MONEY DRAWING OIL

HIGH JOHN THE CONQUEROR

This soap is used to conquer and
dominate your enemies.
1 CUP HIGH JOHN THE CONQUEROR
ROOT POWDER
2 TBLSP. PWDRD. PALO VENCE
BATALLA
1 TBLSP. PWDRD. PALO AMARGO
1 TBLSP. DRAGON'S BLOOD PWDR.
21 DROPS HIGN JOHN THE
CONQUEROR OIL
10 DROPS BLACK PEPPER OIL
7 DROPS MANDRAKE OIL

LUCKY GAMBLER'S SOAP

This soap is used to bring gambling
luck to an individual.
1 TBLSP. CLOVE
1 TBLSP. NUTMEG
1 TBLSP. ALLSPICE
1 TBLSP. ABRE CAMINO HERB
1 TBLSP. BOTON DE ORO HERB
10 DROPS PATCHOULI OIL
7 DROPS PINE OIL
7 DROPS JASMINE OIL

DRAGON'S BLOOD SOAP

This soap is used for protection and
to banish negativity.
1 CUP DRAGON'S BLOOD POWDER
1 TBLSP. MANDRAKE ROOT PWDR.
1 TBLSP. RUE
1 TBLSP. SAGE
30 DROPS DRAGON'S BLOOD OIL

REVERSE EVIL EYE SOAP

This soap is used to reverse a
spiritual attack.
1 CUP RUE
1 TBLSP. CASCARILLA
(EGGSHELL POWDER)
1 TBLSP. GARLIC
1 TBLSP. SAGE
1 TBLSP. SANDALWOOD PWDR.
10 DROPS REVERSE OIL
10 DROPS RUE OIL

COME TO ME SOAP

This soap is used to attract and
dominate an individual.
1 TBLSP. PWDRD. PALO VEN A MI
1 TBLSP. PWDRD. PARA MI
1 TBLSP. VIOLETS
1 TBLSP. CINNAMON PWDR.
10 DROPS PEPPERMINT OIL
10 DROPS PATCHOULY OIL
7 DROPS LILAC OIL

PUERTO RICAN SPIRITUALISTS SOAP

This soap is used to bring an indi-
vidual prosperity,success and luck.
1 CUP ROSES
1 TBLSP. CINNAMON
1 TBLSP. VIOLETS
1 TBLSP. RUE
1 TBLSP. ABRE CAMINO HERB
10 DROPS ROSE OIL
7 DROPS LAVENDER OIL
10 DROPS MINT OIL

CLEOPATRA LOVE SOAP

This soap is used by women to
attract a man.
1 TBLSP. CINNAMON POWDER
1 TBLSP. PWDRD. PALO VEN A MI
1 TBLSP. PWDRD. PALO AMANSA
GUAPO
7 DROPS WANG YLANG OIL
7 DROPS AMBERGRIS OIL
10 DROPS CINNAMON OIL
21 DROPS SECRETS OF CLEOPATRA
PERFUME

MONTENEGRO PALO MAYOMBE
SPECIAL CLEANSING SOAP

My own formula for cleansing an individual from the evil eye. This soap will also protect an individual from powerful black magic spiritual attacks. This soap should be used by an individual for 9 consecutive days and then followed by a series of Sweet Herb Soaps.

1. *1 tblsp. Ache De Santo Herbs*
2. *1 tblsp. pwdrd.*
   Palo Vence Batalla
3. *1 tblsp. Deerhorn powder*
4. *1 tblsp. Dragon's Blood pwdr.*
5. *1 tblsp. pwdrd. Palo Caballero*
6. *1 tblsp. powdered Black Dog Bone (Head and legs)*
7. *1 tblsp. pwdrd. Human Bone (Head, legs and hands)*
8. *10 drops Sage Oil*
9. *7 drops Rue Oil*
10. *2 drops Frankincense Oil*
11. *2 drops Myrrh Oil*
12. *7 drops Camphor Oil*
13. *7 drops Coconut Oil*
14. *10 drops Dragon's Blood Oil*

16

MAGICAL
BODY LOTIONS

Body Lotions are a great way to anoint yourself with magical properties. Body Lotions can be applied daily after taking a ritual bath to ensure the maximum benefit of your desires.

THE GENERAL FORMULA FOR
MAKING SCENTED BODY LOTIONS

• *Place one cup of unscented body lotion or*
body cream in a mixing bowl.
• *Add all of the oils in the bowl.*
• *Mix well and place the Body Lotion in a*
storage jar until ready to use.

ROSE BODY LOTION
40 DROPS ROSE OIL

LILAC BODY LOTION
40 DROPS LILAC OIL

LAVENDER BODY LOTION
40 DROPS LAVENDER OIL

RUE BODY LOTION
40 DROPS RUE OIL

ROSEMARY BODY LOTION
40 DROPS ROSEMARY OIL

CINNAMON BODY LOTION
40 DROPS CINNAMON OIL

SEVEN AFRICAN POWERS
5 DROPS ALLSPICE OIL
5 DROPS AMBERGRIS OIL
10 DROPS CINNAMON OIL
10 DROPS MUSK OIL
10 DROPS COCONUT OIL

ELEGGUA SUCCESS
20 DROPS COCONUT OIL
10 DROPS HEATHER OIL
10 DROPS NUTMEG OIL

ELEGGUA MONEY DRAWING
20 DROPS COCONUT OIL
15 DROPS PEPPERMINT OIL
5 DROPS ANISE OIL

ELEGGUA REVERSE
10 DROPS SPEARMINT OIL
10 DROPS AMBROSIA OIL
5 DROPS COFFEE OIL
10 DROPS COCONUT OIL
5 DROPS ORRIS OIL

OBATALA PURIFICATION
20 DROPS COCONUT OIL
5 DROPS SAGE OIL
5 DROPS EUCALYPTUS OIL
10 DROPS ASTER OIL

OBATALA PEACE
30 DROPS COCONUT OIL
20 DROPS FRANKINCENSE OIL

YEMAYA FERTILITY
10 DROPS COCONUT OIL
10 DROPS CRYSANTHEMUM OIL
20 DROPS WATERMELON OIL

YEMAYA PROTECTION
10 DROPS COCONUT OIL
10 DROPS LILAC OIL
10 DROPS HYACINTH OIL
10 DROPS ASTER OIL

OCHUN LOVE
20 DROPS CINNAMON OIL
5 DROPS AMBERGRIS OIL
10 DROPS HONEY OIL
5 DROPS ROSE OIL

OCHUN MONEY DRAWING
10 DROPS CINNAMON OIL
20 DROPS LAVENDER OIL
10 DROPS LOTUS OIL

CHANGO VICTORY
20 DROPS DRAGON'S BLOOD OIL
10 DROPS AMBERGRIS OIL
5 DROPS SANDALWOOD OIL
5 DROPS HYSSOP OIL

CHANGO LOVE
20 DROPS APRICOT OIL
5 DROPS BASIL OIL
10 DROPS HISBISCUS OIL
10 DROPS CLOVE OIL

OCHOSI PROTECTION
10 DROPS PEONY OIL
10 DROPS PINE OIL
20 DROPS ALLSPICE OIL

SAN LAZARO HEALING
5 DROPS SAGE OIL
10 DROPS WINTERGREEN OIL
10 DROPS LIME OIL
15 DROPS COCONUT OIL

ORUNLA DIVINATION
10 DROPS ACACIA OIL
10 DROPS YLANG YLANG OIL
5 DROPS WISTERIA OIL
5 DROPS JASMINE OIL
5 DROPS PEPPERMINT OIL
5 DROPS COCONUT OIL

SPIRITUALIST'S BODY LOTION
20 DROPS COCONUT OIL
10 DROPS EVERGREEN OIL
5 DROPS CAMPHOR OIL
5 DROPS MISTLETOE OIL

AQUARIUS
20 DROPS PATCHOULY OIL
10 DROPS LAVENDER OIL
5 DROPS PEPPERMINT OIL
5 DROPS ACACIA OIL

LIBRA
20 DROPS VANILLA OIL
10 DROPS ROSE OIL
5 DROPS PLUMERIA OIL
5 DROPS LILAC OIL

ARIES
20 DROPS CARNATION OIL
5 DROPS JUNIPER OIL
10 DROPS CINNAMON OIL
5 DROPS DRAGON'S BLOOD OIL

CANCER
20 DROPS VIOLET OIL
10 DROPS LILAC OIL
5 DROPS AMBERGRIS OIL
5 DROPS LEMON OIL

GEMINI
20 DROPS LAVENDER OIL
10 DROPS LILY OIL
5 DROPS PEPPERMINT OIL
5 DROPS ALMOND OIL

CAPRICORN
20 DROPS PATCHOULY OII
5 DROPS VERTIVERT OIL
10 DROPS HONEYSUCKLE OIL
5 DROPS CYPRESS OIL

LEO
20 DROPS AMBERGRÍS OIL
10 DROPS CINNAMON OIL
10 DROPS MUSK OIL

PISCES
10 DROPS NUTMEG OIL
10 DROPS JASMINE OIL
5 DROPS ANISE OIL
15 DROPS HONEYSUCKLE OIL

SAGITTARIUS
30 DROPS ROSE OIL
5 DROPS GINGER OIL
S DROPS CEDARWOOD OIL

TAURUS
20 DROPS VIOLET OIL
10 DROPS ROSE OIL
5 DROPS VANILLA OIL
5 DROPS LILAC OIL

VIRGO
20 DROPS LAVENDER OIL
10 DROPS LILY OIL
5 DROPS BERGAMOT OIL
5 DROPS HONEYSUCKLE OIL

SCORPIO
20 DROPS VIOLET OIL
5 DROPS AMBERGRIS OIL
5 DROPS CLOVE OIL
10 DROPS GARDENIA OIL

COME TO ME
20 DROPS CINNAMON OIL
10 DROPS YLANG YLANG OIL
5 DROPS AMBERGRIS OIL
5 DROPS VANILLA OIL

GET RID OF EVIL
20 DROPS DRAGON'S BLOOD OIL
10 DROPS PEPPERMINT OIL
5 DROPS ANGELICA OIL
5 DROPS MISTLETOE OIL

SPELL BREAKER
20 DROPS SANDALWOOD OIL
10 DROPS MYRRH OIL
10 DROPS LILAC OIL

LUCKY DICE GAMBLING
20 DROPS JASMINE OIL
10 DROPS PATCHOULY OIL
10 DROPS CINNAMON OIL

PROSPERITY
20 DROPS VIOLET OIL
10 DROPS ROSE OIL
5 DROPS CINNAMON OIL
5 DROPS PINE OIL

BETTER BUSINESS
20 DROPS HEATHER OIL
10 DROPS HYSSOP OIL
5 DROPS VIOLET OIL
5 DROPS COCONUT OIL

QUICK MARRIAGE
10 DROPS AMBERGRIS OIL
10 DROPS PEPPERMINT OIL
10 DROPS LAVENDER OIL
10 DROPS VANILLA OIL

BANISHING
10 DROPS MYRRH OIL
10 DROPS FRANKINCENSE OIL
10 DROPS PEPPERMINT OIL
10 DROPS DRAGON'S BLOOD OIL

DRAGON'S BLOOD
30 DROPS DRAGON'S BLOOD OIL
10 DROPS MUSK OIL

COURT VICTORY
10 DROPS CAMPHOR OIL
10 DROPS SAGE OIL
20 DROPS NUTMEG OIL

DOMINATION
20 DROPS YLANG YLANG OIL
10 DROPS VIOLET OIL
10 DROPS VANILLA OIL

FAST MONEY
10 DROPS CINNAMON OIL
20 HYSSOP OIL
5 DROPS NUTMEG OIL
5 DROPS HONEYSUCKLE OIL

FAST LUCK
20 DROPS PATCHOULY OIL
5 DROPS PINE OIL
10 DROPS VERTIVERT OIL
5 DROPS CINNAMON OIL

ATTRACTION
25 DROPS VANILLA OIL
10 DROPS TUBEROSE OIL
5 DROPS ROSEMARY OIL

LUCKY LOTTO
10 DROPS SAGE OIL
5 DROPS CIVET OIL
10 DROPS ALLSPICE OIL
15 DROPS CLOVER OIL

UNCROSSING
10 DROPS FRANKINCENSE OIL
10 DROPS SAGE OIL
5 DROPS MYRRH OIL
10 DROPS COCONUT OIL
5 DROPS LILAC OIL

JUST JUDGE
20 DROPS MANDRAKE OIL
10 DROPS DRAGON'S BLOOD OIL
5 DROPS HYACINTH OIL
5 DROPS RUE OIL

LOVE DROPS
20 DROPS CINNAMON OIL
10 DROPS VANILLA OIL
10 DROPS PATCHOULY OIL

REVERSIBLE
10 DROPS BASIL OIL
10 DROPS PINE OIL
10 DROPS GINGER OIL
10 DROPS DRAGON'S BLOOD OIL

PURIFICATION
20 DROPS COCONUT OIL
10 DROPS PEPPERMINT OIL
5 DROPS NUTMEG OIL
5 DROPS CINNAMON OIL

HUMMINGBIRD LOVE
20 DROPS HONEYSUCKLE OIL
10 DROPS PLUMERIA OIL
5 DROPS ROSE OIL
5 DROPS LILAC OIL

LAW STAY AWAY
10 DROPS ANISE OIL
10 DROPS HYSSOP OIL
10 DROPS SAGE OIL
10 DROPS HONEYSUCKLE OIL

HIGH JOHN THE CONQUEROR
20 DROPS HIGH JOHN THE
CONQUEROR OIL
5 DROPS YLANG YLANG OIL
5 DROPS CINNAMON OIL
10 DROPS LAVENDER OIL

17

TINCTURES

Tinctures are alcohol based extracts which can be used to make powerful perfumes, colognes and spiritual waters. By adding a small amount of tincture to a magical perfume or cologne, the results will be increased. Tinctures are a great way to empower commercially produced products. By using the following formula, you will be able to produce hundreds of specially prepared tinctures. Each tincture has its own magical quality and usage. I have included just a few recipes that I use in magical preparations for my clients. All of the following tinctures are for cosmetic use only and are not to be consumed or used for medicinal purposes.

THE GENERAL FORMULA FOR MAKING TINCTURES

- *Place 2 cups of 151 proof Bacardi Rum in a glass bottle*
- *Add all of the ingredients into the rum.*
- *Seal the jar and store for 21 days in a darkened location.*
- *If you will be making a tincture from one specific type of herb, add 1 cup herb to 2 cups 151 Rum.*

BITTER HERB TINCTURE
This tincture is used to remove negative vibrations.
1 TBLSP. FRESH SAGE
1 TBLSP. FRESH RUE
1 TBLSP. DRAGON'S BLOOD POWDER
1 TBLSP. LIMES

SWEET HERB TINCTURE
This tincture is used to bring prosperity and luck.
1 TBLSP. FRESH MINT LEAVES
1 TBLSP. CINNAMON STICKS
1 TBLSP. ROSE PETALS
1 TBLSP. LILAC FLOWERS

ABRE CAMINO TINCTURE

This tincture is used to open up the roads of opportunity and success.

2 TBLSP. ABRE CAMINO HERB
1/4 CUP PALO ABRE CAMINO
1 TABLESPOON NUTMEG POWDER

QUITA MALDICION TINCTURE

This tincture is used to get rid of negativity and enemies.

1/4 CUP PALO QUITA MALDICION
2 TBLSP. QUITA MALDICION HERB
1 TBLSP. DRAGON'S BLOOD POWDER

AZUCENA TINCTURE

This tincture is used to attract love and marriage.

1 CUP AZUCENA FLOWERS
2 TBLSP. CINNAMON STICKS
1/4 CUP WATER LILY PETALS

AMANSA GUAPO TINCTURE

This tincture is used to bring love and to attract wealth.

2 TBLSP. AMANSA GUAPO HERB
1/4 CUP PALO AMANSA GUAPO
1/4 CUP PALO BRAZIL

RUE TINCTURE

This tincture is used to protect an individual from the evil eye.

1 CUP FRESH RUE
1/4 CUP PALO VENCE BATALLA
1 TBLSP. DEERHORN POWDER

ALBAHACA TINCTURE

This tincture is used to get rid of the evil eye.

1 CUP FRESH ALBAHACA
2 TBLSP. SAGE
1 TBLSP. KOSHER ROCK SALT

COCONUT TINCTURE

This tincture is used for protection and blessings.

1/4 CUP GUAYABA LEAVES
1/4 CUP SHREDDED COCONUT
1 TBLSP. ABRE CAMINO HERB

ACHE DE SANTO TINCTURE

This tincture is used for blessings, protection and supernatural power.

2 TBLSP. ACHE DE SANTO HERBS
2 TBLSP. ABRE CAMINO HERBS
1 TBLSP. BOTON DE ORO HERB
1/4 CUP PEPPERMINT LEAVES

BRAZILIAN MACUMBA

This tincture is used for general magical purposes.

1 TBLSP. ABRE CAMINO HERB
1 TBLSP. GUARANA HERB
1 TBLSP. PWDRD. PALO COCUYO
1 TBLSP. PWDRD. PALO AMARGO

ESPANTA MUERTO TINCTURE

This tincture is used to banish an evil spirit from an individual.

1 CUP ESPANTA MUERTO HERB
2 TBLSP. PWDRD. PALO ESPANTA MUERTO
1/4 CUP FRESH GARLIC

ESPANTA POLICIA TINCTURE

This tincture is used to protect an individual from the law.

3 TBLSP. PWDRD. PALO ESPANTA POLICIA
2 TBLSP. DEERHORN POWDER
1 HIGH JOHN THE CONQUEROR ROOT
1 MANDRAKE ROOT

SEVEN AFRICAN POWERS

This tincture is used for blessings, protection and success.

1/4 CUP MINT LEAVES
1 TBLSP. RUE
1 TBLSP. SAGE
1TBLSP. EUCALYPTUS
1 TBLSP. ABRE CAMINO HERB
3 STICKS OF CINNAMON
1 TBLSP. HONEY
1 TBLSP. AUZUCENA FLOWERS
1 TBLSP. LAVENDER FLOWERS

ELEGGUA'S REVERSE TINCTURE

This tincture is used to reverse a
spiritual attack.
2 TBLSP. PWDRD. PALO GUAYABA
3 STICKS OF PALO CABALLERO
1 /4 CUP GARDENIA FLOWERS
1 TBLSP. PICA PICA
1 TBLSP. SAGE
1 TBLSP. RUE
1 MANDRAKE ROOT

ELEGGUA'S SUCCESS TINCTURE

This tincture is used to bring success
and opportunity to an individual.
1/4 CUP ABRE CAMINO HERB
1 TBLSP. FRESH SHREDDED COCONUT
1/4 CUP VIOLET FLOWERS
1/4 CUP MARIGOLD FLOWERS
1/4 CUP HEATHER FLOWERS

OCHUN'S LOVE TINCTURE

This tincture is used in love and
marriage spells.
1/4 CUP AMANSA GUAPO HERB
1 TBLSP. PWDRD. PALO VEN A MI
1/4 CUP CINNAMON STICKS
1/4 CUP PACHOULY ROOTS

CHANGO'S DOMINATION

This tincture is used by men to
attract women.
1/4 CUP PARAISO HERB
2 TBLSP. DRAGON'S BLOOD PWDR.
1 TBLSP. JUNIPER
1 TBLSP. SAGE
1 TBLSP. PWDRD. PALO
  AMANSA GUAPO

CHANGO'S DESTRUCTION

This tincture is used to destroy an
individual.
1/4 CUP STICKS OF PALO VENCE
  BATALLA
2 TBLSP. PWDRD. PALO CAMBIA
  RUMBA
2 TBLSP. PWDRD. PALO MUERTO
1 STICK OF PALO PINO

YEMAYA'S PEACE TINCTURE

This tincture is used to bring
peace and tranquility.
1/4 CUP SEAWEED
1 TBLSP. CASCARILLA
(EGGSHELL POWDER)
2 TBLSP. SHREDDED COCONUT
7 STICKS PALO DULCE
1 TBLSP. SEA SALT

YEMAYA'S FERTILITY

This tincture is used by women
for fertility.
1/4 PASSION FLOWERS
1 TBLSP. SEAWEED
1 TBLSP. SANDALWOOD PWDR.
3 TBLSP. BASIL
1/4 CUP GARDENIA FLOWERS

OBATALA'S PURIFICATION

This tincture is used to purify an
individual from negative vibrations.
1/4 CUP WHITE ROSE PETALS
1/4 CUP WHITE CARNATION PETALS
1/4 CUP GARDENIA PETALS
1/4 CUP EUCALYPTUS LEAVES
2 TBLSP. SHREDDED COCONUT

SAN LAZARO'S HEALING

This tincture is used to heal
and prevent illness.
1/4 CUP CINNAMON STICKS
1/4 CUP MINT
1/2 TBLSP. CAMPHOR
1/4 CUP EUCALYPTUS LEAVES
1/4 CUP BAY LEAVES

OCHOSI'S COURT VICTORY

This tincture is used to bring
victory in court.
1/4 CUP ANISE
1/4 CUP QUITA MALDICION HERB
2 TBLSP. DEERHORN PWDR.
1/4 CUP ABRE CAMINO HERB
3 STICKS PALO JOBOVAN

MONEY DRAWING
This tincture is used to bring fast money to an individual.
1/4 CUP PACHOULY ROOTS
1/4 CUP ABRE CAMINO HERB
2 TBLSP. CINNAMON POWDER
1/4 CUP HIGH JOHN THE CONQUEROR ROOTS

PURIFICATION TINCTURE
This tincture is used to bring clarity of mind.
1/4 CUP FRANKINCENSE
1/4 CUP MYRRH
2 TBLSP. SAGE
1/4 CUP PEPPERMINT

HIGH JOHN THE THE CONQUEROR
This tinchure is used to bring an individual power and protection.
1 CUP HIGH JOHN THE CONQUEROR ROOTS
2 TBLSP. DRAGON'S BLOOD POWDER
1 TBLSP. CLOVE
1 TBLSP. CINNAMON POWDER

COME TO ME TINCTURE
This tincture is used to attract an individual for love.
1 CUP STICKS OF PALO VEN A MI
1/4 CUP PARA MI HERB
1/4 CUP VEN A MI HERB
1/4 CUP VENCEDOR HERB
1 TBLSP. PALO LLAMAO
1/4 CUP CINNAMON STACKS

DRAGON'S BLOOD TINCTURE
This tincture is used for protection and to remove negative vibrations.
1 CUP DRAGON'S BLOOD POWDER
1/4 CUP VENCEDOR HERB
1/4 CUP QUINTA MALDICION HERB

CONFLICT TINCTURE
This tincture is used to bring conflict between individuals.
1 BLACK BAT
1 TBLSP. PWDRD. PALO MUERTO
1 TBLSP. PWDRD. PALO CAMBIA RUMBA
1 TBLSP. PWDRD. PALO OJANCHO
1 TBLSP. PWDRD. BLACK CAT BONES
1 TBLSP. PWDRD. BLACK DOG BONES
1 TBLSP. PWDRD. FIGHTING COCKS SPUR

ROSE TINCTURE
This tincture is used for luck and success.
1/4 CUP RED ROSE PETALS
1/4 CUP WHITE ROSE PETALS
1/4 CUP YELLOW ROSE PETALS
1/4 CUP CINNAMON STICKS

CINNAMON TINCTURE
This tincture is used to bring love and luck to an individual.
1 CUP CINNAMON STICKS
1/4 CUP CINNAMON POWDER
1 TBLSP. AMANSA GUAPO HERB
1 TBLSP. PWDRD. PALO DULCE

18

PERFUMES & COLOGNES

Making magical perfumes and natural colognes for my clients is perhaps one of my favorite activities. Perfumes when prepared in the correct fashion can be worn as part of a magical spell or ritual. Making these magical scents is an easy simple process, effective and magical.

THE GENERAL FORMULA FOR MAKING PERFUMES AND COLOGNES

- *Add 2 cups of Cosmetic Alcohol S.D. (40 Proof) to a glass bottle.*
- *Mix all of ingredients with the alcohol.*
- *Seal the bottle and store for 7 days before using.*
- *If desired, add a few drops (DRP.) of your favorite cologne or perfume.*

ABRE CAMINO COLOGNE
21 DRP. ABRE CAMINO TINCTURE
30 DRP. CINNAMON TINCTURE
20 DRP. ROSE TINCTURE
14 DRP. GARDENIA FLOWER TINCT.

AMANSA GUAPO COLOGNE
30 DRP. AMANSA GUAPO HERB TINCT.
35 DRP. CINNAMON TINCTURE
21 DRP. PALO VEN A MI TINCTURE
5 DRP. PALO BRAZIL TINCTURE

AZUCENA PERFUME
40 DRP. AZUCENA FLOWER TINCT.
25 DR. CINNAMON TINCTURE
25 DRP. LAVENDER FLOWER TINCT.
7 DRP. ABRE CAMINO HERB TINCT.

QUITA MALDICION COLOGNE
40 DRP. QUITA MALDIC. HERB TINCT.
20 DRP. RUE TINCTURE
10 DRP. SAGE TINCTURE
5 DRP. DRAGON'S BLOOD TINCT.

ESPANTA MUERTO COLOGNE
40 DRP. ESPANTA MUERTO HERB
TINCTURE
20 DRP. PALO ESPANTA MALDICION
TINCTURE
10 DRP. DRAGON'S BLOOD TINCTURE
5 DRP. CAMPHOR TINCTURE

ESPANTA POLICIA COLOGNE
30 DRP. PALO ESPANTA POLICIA
TINCTURE
15 DRP. ANISE TINCTURE
20 DRP. HIGH JOHN THE
CONQUEROR TINCTURE
21 DRP. DEERHORN PWDR. TINCTURE

ACHE DE SANTO COLOGNE
40 DRP. ACHE DE SANTO TINCTURE
20 DRP. ABRE CAMINO TINCTURE
5 DRP. CAMPOR TINCTURE
10 DRP. CINNAMON TINCTURE
25 DRP. ROSE TINCTURE

VEN A MI PERFUME
30 DRP. PALO VEN A MI TINCTURE
25 DRP. CINNAMON TINCTURE
15 DRP. LAVENDER TINCTURE
25 DRP. AMANSA GUANO TINCTURE

OVERCOME YOUR ENEMIES COLOGNE
25 DRP. PALO VENCE BATALLA
TINCTURE
20 DRP. PALO AMARGO TINCTURE
20 DRP. DRAGON'S BLOOD TINCTURE

PATCHOULY PERFUME
40 DRP. PATCHOULY TINCTURE
20 DRP. CINNAMON TINCTURE
25 DRP. LILAC TINCTURE
25 DRP. LAVANDER TINCTURE

SEVEN AFRICAN POWERS PERFUME
25 DRP. MINT TINCTURE
25 DRP. PEPPERMINT TINCTURE
21 DRP. BOTON DE ORO HERB
TINCTURE
21 DRP. PARAISO HERB TINCTURE
21 DRP. ABRE CAMINO HERB TINCTURE

ELEGGUA PROSPERITY COLOGNE
30 DRP. COCONUT TINCT.
20 DRP. ABRE CAMINO HERB TINCT.
25 DRP. BOTON DE ORO HERB TINCT.
25 DRP. ROSE OF JERICHO TINCT.

OCHUN LOVE PERFUME
30 DRP. CINNAMON TINCT.
25 DRP. PASSION FLOWER TINCT.
15 DRP. HONEYSUCKLE FLWR. TINCT.
21 DRP. AMANSA GUAPO TINCT.
10 DRP. DAMIANA HERB TINCT.

YEMAYA PEACE PERFUME
25 DRP. ANIL TINCT.
10 DRP. SEAWEED TINCT.
10 DRP. LAVENDER FLOWER TINCT.

CHANGO'S VICTORY COLOGNE
25 DRP. PARAISO HERB TINCTURE
10 DRP. PALO VENCE BATALLA
TINCTURE
15 DRP. CINNAMON TINCTURE
15 DRP. QUITA MALDIC. HERB TINCT.

OYA'S PROTECTION PERFUME
25 DRP. MARIGOLD FLOWERS TINCT.
10 DRP. FLOR DE CEMETERIO HERB
TINCTURE
15 DRP. PALO COCUYO TINCTURE
15 DRP. PALO GUAMO TINCTURE
15 DRP. DEERHORN POWDER TINCT.

OBATALA'S PURIFICATION COLOGNE
10 DRP. EUCALYPTUS TINCTURE
10 DRP. SAGE TINCTURE
10 DRP. RUE TINCTURE
30 DRP. COCONUT TINCTURE

SAN LAZARO'S HEALING COLOGNE
30 DRP. BAY LEAF TINCTURE
30 DRP. COCONUT TINCTURE
20 DRP. QUITA MALDICION HERB TINCT.
20 DRP. ESPANTA MUERTO HERB TINCT.
5 DRP. EUCALYPTUS TINCTURE
15 DRP. CINNAMON TINCTURE

REVERSE EVIL PERFUME
25 DRP. DRAGON'S BLOOD TINCTURE
10 DRP. RUE TINCTURE
10 DRP. FRANKINCENSE TINCTURE
10 DRP. MYRRH TINCTURE

PROSPERITY PERFUME
25 DRP. ABRE CAMINO HERB TINCT.
20 DRP. PARAISO HERB TINCTURE
20 DRP. HIGH JOHN THE
CONQUEROR ROOT TINCTURE
25 DRP. CINNAMON TINCTURE

FAST LUCK PERFUME
40 DRP. PALO NAMO TINCTURE
25 DRP. PALO GUAYABA TINCTURE
10 DRP. ROSE TINCTURE
25 DRP. PATCHOULY ROOT TINCT.
15 DRP. PEPPERMINT TINCTURE

MONEY DRAWING PERFUME
25 DRP. CÍNNAMON TINCTURE
15 DRP. ABRE CAMINO HERB TINCT.
15 DRP. BOTON DE ORO TINCTURE
10 DRP. NUTMEG TINCTURE

LUCKY GAMBLER'S COLOGNE
25 DRP. FIVE FINGER GRASS TINCT.
20 DRP. PATCHOULY ROOT TINCT.
15 DRP. MINT LEAF TINCTURE
15 DRP. PEPPERMINT LEAF TINCT.

APHORDISIAC COLOGNE
30 DRP. PASSION FLOWER TINCT.
10 DRP. AMBERGRIS TINCTURE
20 DRP. CINNAMON TINCTURE
15 DRP. MUSK TINCTURE

ESCAPE THE LAW COLOGNE
30 DRP. DEERHORN POWDER TINCT.
20 DRP. PALO ESPAN. POLICIA
TINCTURE
15 DRP. PALO VENCE BATALLA
TINCTURE
15 DRP. LILAC TINCTURE

DOMINATION PERFUME
35 DRP. 7 AFRICAN POWERS TINCT.
20 DRP. CINNAMON TINCTURE
10 DRP. PALO CABALLERO TINCT.
10 DRP. SANDALWOOD TINCTURE

MONTENEGRO LOVE PERFUME
25 DRP. ROSEMARY TINCTURE
10 DRP. GUARANA HERB TINCT.
10 DRP. LAVENDER TINCTURE
5 DRP. MINT LEAF TINCTURE
5 DRP. LILAC FLOWER TINCTURE
10 DRP. ABRE CAMINO HERB TINCT.
15 DRP. COME TO ME TINCTURE

PALO MAYOMBE PROTECTION COLOGNE
25 DRP. PALO ESPANTA MUERTO
TINCT.
25 DRP. PALO VENCE BATALLA TINCT.
5 DRP. CAMPHOR TINCTURE
5 DRP. DRAGON'S BLOOD TINCT.
15 DRP. HIGH JOHN THE CONQ.TINCT.
10 DRP. HUMAN BONE TINCT.
(HEAD AND LEGS)

AQUARIUS COLOGNE
20 DROPS PEPPERMINT TINCTURE
25 DROPS PINE TINCTURE
10 DROPS LAVENDER TINCTURE
10 DROPS ACACIA TINCTURE

ARIES COLOGNE
25 DRP. CARNATION FLWR. TINCT.
15 DRP. CINNAMON TINCT.
10 DRP. FRANKINCENSE TINCT.
5 DRP. MUSK TINCT.

VIRGO COLOGNE
25 DRP. HONEYSUCKLE FLWR. TINCT.
15 DRP. PEPPERMINT LEAF TINCT.
10 DRP. LAVENDER FLWR. TINCT.
5 DRP. PATCHOULY ROOT TINCT.

TAURUS COLOGNE
25 DRP. VIOLET FLWR. TINCT.
20 DRP. ROSE PETAL TINCT.
10 DRP. LILAC FLOWER TINCT.
10 DRP. ORCHID FLOWER TINCT.

GEMINI COLOGNE
25 DRP. LEMONGRASS TINCT.
20 DRP. PEPPERMINT LEAF TINCT.
15 DRP. LAVENDER FLWR. TINCT.
15 DRP. ANISE FLWR. TINCT.

CANCER COLOGNE
10 DRP. EUCALYPTUS
15 DRP. GARDENIA FLWR. TINCT.
20 DRP. ROSE PETAL FLWR. TINCT.
10 DRP. SANDALWOOD FLWR. TINCT.
5 DRP. VIOLET FLOWER FLWR. TINCT.

LEO COLOGNE
10 DRP. FRANKINCENSE TINCTURE
20 DRP. MUSK TINCTURE
15 DRP. ORANGE PEAL TINCTURE
25 DRP. CINNAMON TINCTURE
5 DRP. JUNIPER TINCTURE

LIBRA COLOGNE
25 DRP. ROSE TINCTURE
15 DRP. SPEARMINT LEAF TINCTURE
10 DRP. VANILLA TINCTURE
10 DRP. LILAC TINCTURE

SCORPIO COLOGNE
15 DRP. CLOVE TINCTURE
25 DRP. VIOLET FLWR. TINCT.
10 DRP. PINE TINCTURE
10 DRP. GARDENIA FLWR. TINCT.
5 DRP. GINGER TINCTURE

SAGITTARIUS COLOGNE
25 DRP. CARNATION FLWR. TINCT.
10 DRP. COPAL TINCTURE
5 DRP. SAGE TINCTURE
15 DRP. DRAGON'S BLOOD TINCTURE
20 DRP. ROSE TINCTURE

PISCES COLOGNE
20 DRP. GARDENIA FLWR. TINCT.
5 DRP. ANISE TINCTURE
5 DRP. SAGE TINCTURE
15 DRP. LEMON PEAL TINCTURE
10 DRP. EUCALYPTUS

CAPRICORN COLOGNE
30 DRP. PATCHOULY ROOT TINCTURE
15 DRP. MAGNOLIA FLWR. TINCT.
15 DRP. CINNAMON TINCTURE
25 DRP. HONEYSUCKLE FLWR. TINCT.

19

SPIRITUAL WATERS

Spiritual waters are used in every ritual aspect by practitioners of Santeria. Spiritual waters are used and created with a variety of ingredients. Every spiritual water has its own magical properties attributed to it. All practitioners of Santeria have their favorite specially prepared magical elixers, here are mine.

THE GENERAL FORMULA FOR
MAKING SPIRITUAL WATERS

- *Pour 3 cups of Holy Water to a large bowl.*
- *Add 1 tablespoon Cascarilla to the bowl.*
- *Mix in all of the ingredients with the liquid mixture.*
- *Store the liquid mixture in a container until ready to use.*

**SPIRITUAL WATER
FOR A SEANCE
(MISA ESPIRITUAL)**
1/4 CUP FLORIDA WATER
1/4 CUP ORANGE WATER
1/4 CUP LAVANDER WATER
1/4 CUP KOLONIA 1800

**SPIRITUAL WATER FOR
SPIRITUAL CLEANSING**
1/2 CUP VIOLET WATER
1/4 CUP COCONUT WATER
1/2 CUP FLORIDA WATER
1/4 CUP KOLONIA 1800
(TOBACCO WATER)
1 TBLSP. KOSHER ROCK SALT

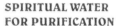

SPIRITUAL WATER
FOR PURIFICATION
1/2 CUP KOLONIA 1800
1/2 CUP SIETE MACHOS COLONGE
1/2 LAVANDER WATER
1/2 CUP ROSE WATER
1/4 CUP BAY RUM SPIRITUAL COLOGNE

SPIRITUAL WATER
FOR CONSECRATION
1/2 CUP FLORIDA WATER
1/4 CUP KOLONIA 1800
1/4 RUE WATER
1/4 CUP BRISAS DEL CARIBE COLOGNE
2 TBLSP. KOSHER ROCK SALT

SPIRITUAL WATER FOR PEACE
1 CUP BAY RUM COLOGNE
1/4 CUP LAVENDER WATER
1 TABLESPOON ANIL POWDER
1/2 CUP SEA WATER
1/2 CUP VIOLET WATER
1/4 CUP COCONUT WATER
1 TABLESPOON SEA SALT

SPIRITUAL WATER
FOR A SPIRITUALIST
1/2 CUP VIOLET WATER
1/2 CUP RIVER WATER
1/2 CUP ROSE WATER
1/2 CUP COCONUT WATER
1 TBLSP. SEA SALT
1 TBLSP. RUE LEAVES
1 TBLSP. PEPPERMINT LEAVES
1/4 CUP ROSE PETALS (WHITE)

SPIRITUAL WATER
FOR GOOD LUCK
1/4 CUP FLORIDA WATER
1/4 CUP SIETE MACHOS COLOGNE
1/4 CUP RHUM QUINQUINA COLOGNE
1/4 CUP KOLONIA 1800
(DOS GARDENIAS)
1/4 CUP CINNAMON STICKS

SPIRITUAL WATER FOR
PROTECTION FROM DEATH
1/4 CUP KOLONIA 1800
(CON VETIVER)
1/4 CUP VIOLET WATER
1/4 CUP SANDALWOOD COLOGNE
1/4 CUP ROSE WATER
1/4 CUP FRESH RUE LEAVES

SPIRITUAL WATER
FOR DREAMING
1 CUP VIOLET WATER
1/4 CUP KANANGA WATER
1/4 CUP SIETE MACHOS COLOGNE
1/4 CUP POMPEY LOTION
1 CUP COCONUT WATER
1/4 CUP VIOLET FLOWERS

SPIRITUAL WATER
FOR LOVE ATTRACTION
1 CUP ROSE WATER
1/4 CUP KOLONÍA 1800
1/4 CUP SIETE MACHOS COLOGNE
1/4 CUP RIVER WATER
1/4 CUP SEA WATER
1/4 CUP POMPEY LOTION
1 CUP ROSE PETALS

20

EARTH
& DIRTS

The use of dirt is an important aspect when making strong amulets or as part of a magical spell. Dirt is used in a variety of different ways such as inside of consecrated Eleggua's, Ozains and other amulets. Both Santeros (Priest of Santeria) and Paleros (Priest of Palo Mayombe) believe that dirt has a magical quality. The following is a list of some of the important and powerful dirts used by participants of the Santeria religion.

DIRT FROM FOUR STREET CORNERS - *This dirt is used to open up the roads of success.*

DIRT FROM THE MOUNTAINS - *This dirt is used in cleansing spells and commmunication with the spirits which reside specifically in a mountain region.*

DIRT FROM THE FOREST - *This dirt is used in spells of protection.*

DIRT FROM FOUR JAILS - *This dirt is used to release an individual from jail or to keep them in.*

DIRT FROM FOUR POLICE STATIONS - *This dirt is used to bring the police to an individuals home or business.*

DIRT FROM FOUR BANKS - *This dirt is used in prosperity spells.*

DIRT FROM AN INDIAN CEMETERY - This dirt is used in spells of protection.

DIRT FROM FOUR CHURCHES - *This dirt is used is cleansing spells.*

DIRT FROM A HOSPITAL - *This dirt is used in cleansing spells or in spells of harm.*

DIRT FROM THE HOME OF A WITCH - *This dirt is used in spells of domination and spells of harm.*

DIRT FROM A SANTERO'S HOME - *This dirt is used in spells of protection.*

DIRT FROM A PALERO'S HOME - *This dirt is used in spells of harm or conflict.*

DIRT FROM A COURT HOUSE - *This dirt is used in court cases to bring victory.*

DIRT FROM 12:00 NOON - *This dirt is used in spells of protection.*

DIRT FROM A HORSE RACETRACK - *This dirt is used in gambling spells.*

DIRT FROM THE SEASHORE - *This dirt is used in fertility and cleansing spells.*

DIRT FROM THE RIVER'S EDGE - *This dirt is used in love spells.*

DIRT FROM THE BOTTOM OF A SHOE - *This dirt is used in spells of domination and harm.*

DIRT FROM WHERE TWO DOG'S HAVE FOUGHT - *This dirt is used in spells to cause conflict.*

DIRT FROM A CASINO - *This dirt is used in money spells.*

DIRT FROM A SOLDIER'S GRAVE - *This dirt is used in spells of protection and domination.*

DIRT FROM A LAW LIBRARY - *This dirt is used in legal matters.*

DIRT FROM A LIBRARTY - *This dirt is used to receive knowledge.*

DIRT FROM A DOCTOR'S OFFICE - *This dirt is used in healing spells.*

MAGICAL SPELLS

TO RELEASE SOMEONE FROM JAIL

1. *Place a photo of the incarcerated individual on a white plate.*
2. *Sprinkle Deerhorn powder and powdered Palo Abre Camino over the photo.*
3. *Place a small metal crossbow of Orisha Ochosi on the photo.*
4. *Sprinkle dirt from the forest over the photo.*
5. *Sprinkle dirt from four jails over the photo.*
6. *Place a red 7 day glass candle next to the plate.*
7. *On the 8th day, wrap the mixture in a white cloth and dispose of it near the jailed individual.*

TO KEEP SOMEONE IN JAIL

1. *Place the phote of the individual on a white plate.*
2. *Sprinkle powdered Palo Cambia Rumba, Palo Justica and Palo Muerto over the photo.*
3. *Sprinkle dirt from four cemeteries over the photo.*
4. *Sprinkle dirt from four police stations over the photo.*
5. *Light a black 7 day glass candle next to the plate.*
6. *On the 8th day, wrap the mixture in a black cloth and bury over a grave.*

TO DOMINATE AN INDIVIDUAL

1. *Place a photo of the individual on a white plate.*
2. *Sprinkle dirt from the bottom of a shoe over the photo.*
3. *Sprinkle dirt from four cemeteries over the photo.*
4. *Light a 7 day glass candle and place it next to the plate.*
5. *On the 8th day, wrap the contents in a red cloth and dispose of it in a wooded area.*

TO CAUSE CONFLICTS

1. *Write the individuals name six times on a brown piece of paper.*
2. *Insert 9 pins through the paper and place it on a white plate.*
3. *Sprinkle black cat and black dog fur over the paper.*
4. *Sprinkle powdered Palo Cambia Rumba and powdered Palo Muerto over the paper.*
5. *Sprinkle dirt from where two dogs have fought over the paper.*
6. *Place a black 7 day glass candle near the plate and then light.*
7. *On the 8th day, wrap the contents and dispose of the contents in a cemetery.*

TO WIN A HORSE RACE

1. *Write the name of the horse three times on a brown piece of paper.*
2. *Sprinkle Deerhorn powder over the paper.*
3. *Sprinkle dirt from four banks over the paper.*
4. *Sprinkle dirt from a horse racetrack over the paper.*
5. *Light a seven colored 7 day glass candle near the plate.*
6. *The candle should burn for three consecutive days before the race.*
7. *On the day of the race, dispose of the contents at a crossroad near the racetrack.*

TO ESCAPE THE LAW

1. *Write your name seven times on a brown piece of paper.*
2. *Place the paper on a white plate.*
3. *Sprinkle Cascarilla (eggshell powder) and Deerhorn powder over the paper.*
4. *Sprinkle dirt from four churches over the name.*
5. *Sprinkle dirt from an Indian cemetery over the paper.*
6. *Light a red 7 day glass candle next to the plate.*
7. *On the 8th day, bury the contents in your yard.*

TO BRING THE POLICE

1. *Place dirt from four police stations, dirt from four street corners, dirt from a court house and dirt from four cemeteries in a mixing bowl.*
2. *Mix all of the dirts together .*
3. *Light a 7-day black candle next to the bowl.*
4. *On the 8th day, sprinkle all of dirts from the bowl at the individuals home or business.*

TO PROTECT YOUR HOME FROM ENEMIES

1. *Mix dirt from the forest, dirt from four churches, dirt from an Indian cemetery, dirt from a Soldiers grave, dirt from a Santero's home and one tablespoon Deerhorn powder together in a large mixing bowl.*
2. *Light a seven colored 7 day candle next to the bowl.*
3. *Recite a prayer to the Seven African Powers daily for seven consecutive days.*
4. *On the 8th day, sprinkle the ingredients around the outside of your home and property.*

TO MAKE AN INDIVIDUAL MOVE

1. *Mix dirt from four cemeteries and dirt from where two dogs have fought together in a mixing bowl.*
2. *Light a seven day black candle next to the mixture.*
3. *Recite the prayer of the Intraquil spirits for seven consecutive days.*
4. *On the 8th day, sprinkle the ingredients on the individuals property.*

Item #222
$11.95

THE PSALM WORKBOOK

by Robert Laremy

Work with the Psalms to Empower, Enrich and Enhance Your Life!

This LARGE PRINT King James version of the Book of Psalms contains nearly 400 simple rituals and procedures that can be used to help you accomplish anything you desire. Use the situational index provided to decide which psalm to pray for your specific need.

**Peace, Protection, Health,
Success, Money, Love,
Faith, Inspiration, Spiritual Strength
And much more!**

Approach your worship with a clean heart and a child-like faith in God's infinite wisdom and you will derive tremendous results from the powers of the psalms.

SPIRITUAL CLEANSINGS & PSYCHIC DEFENSES

By Robert Laremy

Psychic attacks are real and their effects can be devastating to the victim. Negative vibrations can be as harmful as bacteria, germs and viruses. There are time-honored methods of fighting these insidious and pernicious agents of distress. These techniques are described in this book and they can be applied by you. No special training or supernatural powers are needed to successfully employ these remedies. All of the procedures described in this book are safe and effective, follow the instructions without the slightest deviation. The cleansings provided are intended as *"over-the-counter"* prescriptions to be used by anyone being victimized by these agents of chaos.

ISBN 0-942272-72-2 5½"x 8½" 112 pages $9.95

SANTERIA
AFRICAN MAGIC
IN LATIN AMERICA

BY MIGENE GONZALEZ WIPPLER

In 1973, the first hardcover edition of *Santeria: African Magic in Latin America* by cultural anthropologist Migene Gonzalez-Wippler was first published by Julian Press. It became an immediate best-seller and is still considered by many experts one of the most popular books on Santeria, having gone through 4 editions and several translations. Now this beloved classic, written by one the foremost scholars on the Afro-Cuban religion, has returned in a 5th edition. This time the text has been carefully edited and corrected to incorporate vital new material. The beliefs, practices, legends of Santeria are brilliantly brought to life in this exciting and critically acclaimed best-seller. If you ever wondered what Santeria is, if you are curious about the rituals and practices of this mysterious religion, and want to delve in its deepest secrets, this book will answer all your questions and much more.

ISBN 0-942272-04-8 5½"x 8½" $14.95

RITUALS and SPELLS of SANTERÍA

Migene González-Wippler

RITUALS AND SPELLS
OF SANTERIA
Migene Gonzalez Wippler

Santeria is an earth religion. That is, it is a magico-religious system that has its roots in nature and natural forces. Each orisha or saint is identified with a force of nature and with a human interest or endeavor. Chango, for instance, is the god of fire, thunder and lightning, but he is also the symbol of justice and protects his followers against enemies. He also symbolizes passion and virility and is often invoked in works of seduction. Oshun, on the other hand, symbolizes river waters, love and marriage. She is essentially the archetype of joy and pleasure. Yemaya is identified with the seven seas, but is also the symbol of Motherhood and protects women in their endeavors. Eleggua symbolizes the crossroads, and is the orisha of change and destiny, the one who makes things possible or impossible. He symbolizes the balance of things. Obatala is the father, the symbol of peace and purity. Oya symbolizes the winds and is the owner of the cemetery, the watcher of the doorway between life and death. She is not death, but the awareness of its existence. Oggun is the patron of all metals, and protects farmers, carpenters, butchers, surgeons, mechanics, and all who work with or near metals. He also rules over accidents, which he often causes.

ISBN 0-942272-07-2   5½"x 8½" 134 pages $9.95

Item #005

$9.95

POWERS OF THE ORISHAS
Santeria and the Worship of Saints
Migene Gonzalez Wippler

Santeria is the Afro-Cuban religion based on an amalgamation between some of the magio-religious beliefs and practices of the Yoruba people and those of the Catholic church. In Cuba where the Yoruba proliferated extensively, they became known as *Lucumi,* a word that means "friendship".

Santeria is known in Cuba as Lucumi Religion. The original Yoruba language, interspersed with Spanish terms and corrupted through the centuries of misuse and mispronunciation, also became known as Lucumi. Today some of the terms used in Santeria would not be recognized as Yoruba in Southwestern Nigeria, the country of origin of the Yoruba people.

Santeria is a Spanish term that means a confluence of saints and their worship. These saints are in reality clever disguises for some of the Yoruba deities, known as Orishas. During the slave trade, the Yoruba who were brought to Cuba were forbidden the practice of their religion by their Spanish masters. In order to continue their magical and religious observances safely the slaves opted for the identification and disguise of the Orishas with some of the Catholic saints worshipped by the Spaniards. In this manner they were able to worship their deities under the very noses of the Spaniards without danger of punishment.

Throughout the centuries the practices of the Yoruba became very popular and soon many other people of the Americas began to practice the new religion.

ISBN 0-942272-25-0 5½"x 8½" 144 pages $9.95